Broad Peak

Broad Peak

Richard Sale

Translations from German text by
Michaela Gigerl and John Hirst

Carreg

First published in 2004 by
Carreg Limited
18 Parsons Croft
Hildersley, Ross-on-Wye
Herefordshire   HR9 5BN

ISBN 0 9538631 1 5

Acknowledgements
I would like to thank the Schmuck, Wintersteller and Buhl families for their assistance. I thank Qader Saeed and Kurt Diemberger for conversations. I thank Horst Höfler in Germany for his kind assistance, and Monica Gärtner of the Austrian Alpine Association, Innsbruck for her assistance with archive material. In the UK Dieter Pevsner offered invaluable help with all aspects of the book. Finally I would like to thank Nathan Sale for helping to get the best from some of the illustrations.

All reasonable efforts have been made by the Publisher to trace the copyright holder of the photographs which appear on page 22. In the event that a copyright holder comes forward after publication of this edition, the Publisher will endeavour to rectify the position at the earliest opportunity.

The cover has been constructed from two photographs taken by Fritz Wintersteller at the summit. Behind Marcus Schmuck K2 dominates the Karakoram peaks, while to the left is the curving summit ridge from the Forepeak.

Printed and bound in the UK by J W Arrowsmith, Bristol

Contents

Introduction

In the summer of 1957 four young Austrians – Hermann Buhl, Kurt Diemberger, Marcus Schmuck and Fritz Wintersteller – travelled along the Baltoro Glacier on a journey that would take them to the summit of a huge Karakoram peak and into the history books of the sport of mountaineering. Their objective was Broad Peak, the world's twelfth highest mountain, one of the fourteen 8000-metre peaks. The Austrians were planning to climb Broad Peak without the use of either high-altitude porters or bottled oxygen. Though the latter had been achieved before on 8000m peaks, a porter-free ascent had not.

The achievement of a first porter-free, bottled oxygen-free ascent would have been enough to secure the enterprise a place in climbing history, but there was more. One of the team, Hermann Buhl, had climbed Nanga Parbat, the world's ninth-highest peak, in an audacious solo climb from the top camp, a climb which took him 41 hours during which he survived an enforced bivouac with minimal equipment and no food or drink at a height of around 8000m. By all logic Buhl should not have continued with the ascent when it became clear he would have to bivouac on the descent. Logic also suggests he should not have survived the bivouac. Buhl reached the summit and survived the descent. Before Nanga Parbat he was already famous for his climbs. After Nanga Parbat he was a living legend in the climbing world.

Broad Peak from Skil Brum, taken during the ascent of the latter. The line of ascent of Broad Peak and the position of the three camps are marked.

Broad Peak was to be Buhl's second 8000m peak. He would be the second man to achieve that success (after the Sherpa Gyalzen Norbu) but the first to have been on two first ascents (Gyalzen Norbu having been in the first team to summit Manaslu, but having climbed Makalu the day after the first ascent). Broad Peak was also to be Buhl's last summit, as he would die on Chogolisa just days after the summit climb. Buhl's second 8000m peak and subsequent death form part of his legend. Yet by allowing the Broad Peak climb to become just the final chapter in Buhl's life its true significance has been lost. The climb pointed the way to the future. In the immediate aftermath of the Austrian success it seemed that nothing had changed. Gasherbrum I, Dhaulagiri and Shisha Pangma (the last three 8000ers to be climbed) were ascended by large teams using high-altitude porters and, in the case of Gasherbrum I, bottled oxygen. When the next generation of climbers came to the high hills they were intent not on repeating the routes of their predecessors but in climbing harder routes to the same summits – Annapurna's south face, Nanga Parbat's Rupal face, Manaslu's south and north-west faces, Makalu's west pillar. These new ventures required a return to the siege tactics which had brought success to the first summit teams. Then, in 1975, Reinhold Messner from the Italian Tyrol and Austria's Peter Habeler made the second ascent of Gasherbrum I by a new route not only using neither porters nor bottled oxygen, but climbing and descending the mountain in one continuous push over a four-day period from a base camp at 5100m on the Abruzzi Glacier. In completing the climb Messner became the first man to have stood on the summit of three 8000m peaks.

The Habeler-Messner climb was seen as heralding a new era in climbing on the high hills, but in fact it was no more than the logical extension of the Broad Peak climb. In 1957 the four Austrians had hauled 1800kg of equipment to their base camp. In 1975 lightweight equipment and advances in food preparation techniques allowed Habeler and Messner to reduce their total load to 180kg. That 90% reduction enabled them to dispense with the need to stock camps (as the four Austrians had been forced to do), taking everything they needed for the climb in two rucsacs. In climbing time, the final ascent and descent of Broad Peak was accomplished in almost exactly the same time as the Gasherbrum I climb, the difference being that on Broad Peak camps had been established in advance. Later advances in equipment allowed Messner to push the limits of high-altitude climbing even further, soloing Everest using only what he could carry on his back.

The exploits of Messner and later climbers have tended to overshadow the achievements of the Broad Peak team. That the sport of high-altitude climbing has moved on is inevitable: such advances are made in all sports. But what needs to be remembered is just how big an advance the Broad Peak climb was. On the 8000m peaks it took twenty years and the exceptional talents of Messner and Habeler for the rest of the climbing world to catch up. Today the Broad Peak climb seems just one more in the long history of mountaineering, but that is merely another aspect of sporting evolution. Today's master can make yesterday's seem a rather ordinary individual: in turn tomorrow's master will cast today's in the same light.

The Broad Peak climb was pivotal, both in the evolution of climbing and in the evolution of the legend that is Hermann Buhl. Because of Buhl the climb has taken on an almost mythical aura, the great man out in front, leading a small band of admiring disciples to the top of the mountain. But it was not like that. Broad Peak was not Buhl's expedition, neither was he the one on whom success ultimately depended.

In preparing a book on the history of climbing on the 8000m peaks during the 50 years since the ascent of Annapurna, I became aware that information on the Broad Peak climb depended almost exclusively on the account of Kurt Diemberger, the youngest of the four Austrians and the man who had been with Hermann Buhl on the day he fell to his death on Chogolisa. Anxious to ensure that Diemberger's account was an accurate reflection of the climb I corresponded with, then met, Marcus Schmuck and Fritz Wintersteller, who had completed the four-man team. Listening to them and reading their climbing diaries it became clear that the Diemberger account was only one version of this remarkable climb. It was also a version which was at odds with those of the two men who had been the first to reach the summit.

To complete the picture what was also needed was an understanding of Buhl's version of the climbing, but that appeared unlikely as it seemed, frustratingly, that nothing of his account existed. But as research into the climb continued I discovered that in fact it did. Photographs of Buhl on the expedition show him sat on a rock, a typewriter perched on his knees as he taps out his own version of events. Early in his first report of the expedition he notes that 'Right now I'd rather be sitting outside, observing the vivid hustle and bustle of the natives, listening to the twittering of birds and the rustling of the palm trees, or delighting in the rich colours of the local flowers. Instead I sit in a gloomy room and tap away at my typewriter putting down my impressions.' The typed reports were clearly intended to form the basis of a book Buhl was planning on the trip. His book on Nanga Parbat and his climbs leading up to that expedition (translated into English as *Nanga Parbat Pilgrimage*) had been a success and he must have thought that a Broad Peak book would also be a best-seller. If he did then he was probably correct: not only was Buhl a marvellous climber but an excellent writer, his Broad Peak reports showing a more mature touch than is seen in the earlier book. The reports were sent back to his wife in Berchtesgaden where they remained unopened because news of his death made reading them far too painful. The reports surfaced again when Horst Höfler was researching a biography of Buhl (co-produced with Reinhold Messner and published in German in 1997 as *Kompromisslos nach oben*, and in English in 2000 as *Climbing without Compromise*). And, astonishingly, with the reports was a transcript of Buhl's climbing diary. Exactly what happened to the original is, as we shall see, one of the mysteries surrounding the Broad Peak climb, and in its absence it is difficult to know what to make of the transcript. Unsigned and undated it may – but may not – be a true, unedited copy of the original, which would have been hand-written. The provenance of the reports seems more assured. Complete with typing errors and spelling mistakes that a transcriber would surely have corrected and carrying, on one, Buhl's distinctive signature there seems little doubt that they are Buhl's work. Yet they contain passages which are so at odds with the memories of Schmuck and Wintersteller that the latter wrote an angry letter to Höfler after his Buhl biography was published claiming that these passages were fraudulent.

This book draws on the Buhl material and on the diaries of Schmuck and Wintersteller, as well as a conversation with Diemberger and conversations with Qader Saeed, the young Pakistani army officer who was the 'fifth member' of the team.

Schmuck and Wintersteller also had many photographs of the expedition and readily agreed to their use. I had hoped to supplement them with photographs from Diemberger. He is an excellent photographer and his shot of Buhl on Broad Peak's summit is iconic. Unfortunately he declined my request unless I agreed to allow him to check the text before publication. Because of the contentious nature of some of the writings of the other team members I did not feel able to do so. After the return of the three survivors relationships between them were so fraught that the Oesterreichischer Alpenverein, which had co-sponsored the expedition, held a meeting at which they were required to sign a statement indicating that differences had been resolved and that a line had been drawn under the past. It was a valiant, but unsuccessful attempt.

By using all available material the book presents a different and, I would suggest, more complete version of the Broad Peak climb, one in which the four men's roles are presented as they were, rather than as some might wish them to have been.

It must never be forgotten that the Austrian climb was one of the landmarks of mountaineering history and that, whatever friction there was between the four men during the climb and after it, the ascent of Broad Peak stands as a monumental achievement. There are many who consider the Broad Peak climb to be Hermann Buhl's climb. Such a definition is a major injustice to the other members of the team, particularly to the man who was instrumental in putting the expedition together and the man whose indomitable spirit made such a contribution to the final outcome. In publishing this account I hope I have been able to redress the balance a little in their favour.

1
Broad Peak

On Friday, 5 February 1892 a group of men left London's Fenchurch Street railway station on the first leg of a journey that would take them to the head of the Baltoro Glacier in the Karakoram range of mountains. The team was led by William Martin Conway, more an explorer than a climber, a man whose later exploits would include expeditions to Spitsbergen and South America, and would see him become Sir Martin, then Lord, Conway. With Conway were Matthias Zurbriggen, the famous Macugnaga guide whose climbing exploits were later to include the first ascent (solo) of Aconcagua, and Oscar Eckenstein. Eckenstein is credited with the development of the 'modern' crampon and would later (in 1902) lead the first attempt to climb K2 (an expedition that included Aleister Crowley, the self-styled Great Beast 666). Eckenstein was a socialist and hostile to the establishment while Conway was the archetypal establishment man: the pair did not get on. In his book on the expedition Conway notes that before the journey along the Baltoro it was decided that Eckenstein would return to England as 'he had never been well since reaching Gilgit. It was evidently useless for him to come further with us.' The diplomatic language masks serious, and hardly surprising, disagreements between the two men which may have contributed to Eckenstein's problems with British Indian officials at the start of his K2 expedition ten years later.

The photograph of Broad Peak from the north (on the Godwin-Austen Glacier) which appeared in Jules Jacot Guillarmod's book Six Mois dans l'Himalaya, le Karakorum et l'Hindu-Kush.

McCormick's sketch of Broad Peak which appeared in Conway's book Climbing in the Himalayas.

In the Karakoram the team was joined by Charles Bruce, a Gurkha officer who impressed Conway with his enthusiasm and strength, Conway describing him as being like a 'goods train plus engine'. Bruce had been with A.F. Mummery on Nanga Parbat in 1895 and would lead the 1922 and 1924 Everest expeditions, though he was replaced on the latter when he suffered a recurrent bout of malaria. Conway's team followed the Baltoro Glacier to its junction with the Godwin-Austen Glacier flowing down from K2 and the glaciers from the Gasherbrum group of peaks. This point he called the Place de la Concorde 'as a similar place at the head of the Aletsch Glacier is called.' The Aletsch lies in German-speaking Switzerland and the place is therefore more correctly the Concordiaplatz which explains the now-common name – Concordia. Looking towards K2 Conway noted that 'there was a fine breadth of mountain splendour displaying itself on the right of our view – a huge Breithorn, as it were, filling the space between K2 and the hidden Gusherbrum [sic].'

In the Preface to his book Conway notes that 'in the matter of nomenclature I have adhered to Alpine and Caucasian custom. Where a peak has a native name I use it … Native names take precedence and exclude all others. Mountains that have no names I have named myself, for the purpose of this book and map, applying descriptive designations to them and never the names of persons.' Finding no local name, Conway was true to his word, settling on the descriptive name Broad Peak for the mountain that forms the left side of the Godwin-Austen Glacier's valley. Conway's book included a sketch of Broad Peak: photographs of the mountain had to wait until 1902 when Eckenstein's K2 expedition followed the Godwin-Austen Glacier beneath Broad Peak's west flank. Jules Jacot Guillarmod's book on that expedition has photos taken from the north and north-east. Seven years later these were supplemented by a series of shots by Vittorio Sella who accompanied the Duke of Abruzzi's K2 expedition. Sella is regarded by many as the greatest of all mountain photographers: his shots from 1909 that illustrate the expedition book, particularly those of K2 and the panoramas created from series of photographs, have inspired generations of climbers.

The 8000m Peaks

Conway made no attempt to measure Broad Peak's height. In Jacot Guillarmod's book the mountain is referred to as being 'plus de 8500m'. On the Abruzzi expedition Marchese Federico Negrotto measured it at 8270m, but this was reduced to 8047m by a British survey team in 1926. That remains Broad Peak's official height, making it the twelfth highest of the fourteen 8000m peaks.

Attempts to climb the 8000m peaks began in 1895 when the British mountaineers (John) Norman Collie, Geoffrey Hastings and Alfred Mummery attempted Nanga Parbat. Mummery was

A section of the famous panorama by Vittorio Sella. This was Panorama C of Fillipo de Filippi's book of the Abruzzi expedition, La Spedizione nel Karakoram e nell'Imalaia Occidentale 1909, *translated into English as* Karakoram and western Himalaya.

one of the outstanding climbers of the time and with the Gurkha Ragobir Thapa made a determined effort to reach the summit by way of a rock rib on the Diamir face. Thapa became ill at about 6100m ending the attempt, but Mummery was determined to have one more attempt from the north where, he hoped, snow would offer faster progress than rock. He and two Gurkhas disappeared attempting to cross a high pass from the Diamir to the Rakhiot side of the peak.

Ten years after the attempt on Nanga Parbat a British-Swiss team reached about 6500m on Kangchenjunga. Between the 1914–18 and 1939–45 Wars both Nanga Parbat and Kangchenjunga were attempted again, as were Everest, K2 and Gasherbrum I. Several of the Nanga Parbat expeditions ended

in tragedy, one German expedition being virtually wiped out by an avalanche. The Everest trips are famous for the disappearance of Mallory and Irvine in 1924. None of the attempts was successful, though some experts believe that the 1939 attempt on K2 by Fritz Wiessner and the Sherpa Pasang Dawa Lama would have succeeded had the pair chosen the now standard snow route from the top camp rather than a more difficult, and therefore slower, rock route.

In 1950 expeditions to the 8000m peaks, which had been halted by the 1939–45 War, began again, Nepal opening its borders and so adding the remaining 8000m peaks to the list of those available to pre-war expeditions. The French climbed Annapurna at the first attempt, though both the summit climbers suffered dreadful frostbite injuries during an agonising descent. In 1953 Everest and Nanga Parbat were climbed, by British and Austro-German expeditions respectively, each nation seeing a natural justice in their successes in view of earlier defeats and tragedies. K2 was climbed by the Italians in 1954. These expeditions were by large, national teams of climbers supported by local porters, which laid siege to the mountains. The same pattern was followed during the later ascents of Makalu (French 1955: the entire team reached the summit), Kangchenjunga (British 1955), Manaslu (Japanese 1956) and Lhotse (Swiss 1956). The notable exception was the ascent of Cho Oyu in 1954 which was climbed by a three-man Austrian expedition, supported by seven Sherpas. The ascent was also the first post-monsoon climb of an 8000m peak. In 1956 another Austrian expedition made a further advance, the three-man summit team deliberately bivouacing on their way to the summit of Gasherbrum II after the team's Balti porters had declined to make the load carry needed to establish a final camp. Enforced the bivouac may have been, but the climb showed that the techniques of the Alps were now being brought to the highest peaks.

Of the remaining 8000m peaks Gasherbrum I and Dhaulagiri would fall to large teams (of Americans in 1958 and Swiss in 1960 respectively) and siege tactics. Shisha Pangma, the last 8000er to be climbed, in 1964, can certainly be said to have fallen to siege tactics. It was climbed by a Chinese team (the Chinese having occupied Tibet and closed its borders to foreigners) aided by the construction of a road towards the mountain and the erection of a small town (complete with cinema) to house the 200 or so climbers and support workers the ascent involved.

In the list of first ascents, book-ended between the two Gasherbrum peaks, is Broad Peak. The climbs on Cho Oyu and Gasherbrum II had pointed the way, but the Broad Peak ascent was so radically different that it would take a new generation of climbers and a new generation of climbing equipment for it to be equalled.

Early Attempts on Broad Peak

Günter Oscar Dyhrenfurth, leader of the International Himalaya Expedition (IHE) of 1934 which reconnoitred Gasherbrum I, inspected the western and southern sides of Broad Peak looking for potential routes, as he was seriously considering an attempt on the peak. Dyhrenfurth identified a feature he called the 'Western Spur' as the most promising line. Dyhrenfurth noted, though, that this route would be too difficult for Balti porters and that the spur ended short of the col between the main and central summits, an area at high risk from avalanches. Perhaps unconsciously embracing the militarism inherent in the siege approach to expeditions of the time, Dyhrenfurth suggested the use of a mortar to clear the dangerous snow from this area.

When Broad Peak was attempted for the first time Dyhrenfurth's suggestion that the Western Spur would be too difficult for local porters led the expedition leader, Karl-Maria Herrligkoffer, to choose another route. Herrligkoffer was a controversial figure in climbing circles. Born in 1917, he was the half-brother of Willy Merkl who in 1932 led the first German expedition to Nanga Parbat. That expedition, more a reconnaissance than a serious attempt on the peak, had been very successful and so Merkl was given the leadership of a second expedition in 1934. That expedition included Willo Welzenbach, sometime partner of Merkl on Alpine climbs and the finest German-speaking mountaineer of the time. A delay in the climb caused by the death of a team member, probably from oedema, led to the expedition becoming dangerously extended on the mountain. When a storm broke, the retreat turned into a desperate rout during which three Germans, Merkl, Welzenbach and Uli Wieland, together with six Sherpas died. The tragedy remains one of the worst in Himalayan/Karakoram history, both for its death toll and its drawn-out agony.

Herrligkoffer, a general practitioner, was not a climber, but he had hero-worshipped his older brother and was determined to finish the job Merkl had started. In the early 1950s he began to organise an expedition which would follow Merkl's route – a very long line, one no longer favoured by Nanga Parbat

19

aspirants. The attempt was scorned by much of the German climbing establishment and media, but Herrligkoffer showed an admirable doggedness in pursuing his dream, assembling a good team which included: a survivor of the 1934 expedition, the Austrian Peter Aschenbrenner; another Austrian, one acknowledged by many to be the best German-speaking climber of the day, Hermann Buhl; and Kuno Rainer, Buhl's companion on some of his finest climbs. The expedition culminated in a solo climb to the summit by Buhl, a climb which required a bivouac at almost 8000m with minimal equipment. Buhl's right foot was frost-bitten and he subsequently lost the big toe and part of the second toe of that foot.

Nanga Parbat made a mountaineering star of Hermann Buhl, his phenomenal solo climb capturing the imagination of climbers and non-climbers alike. The expedition also made a star of Herrligkoffer, for although doubts were raised over his leadership, these were mainly confined to climbers. To the corporate world Herrligkoffer was a success, and to those climbers happy enough to use his money-gathering skills to further their own desires in the high hills he was a godsend. In 1954, flushed with the success of the previous year, Herrligkoffer wanted to organise a second Karakoram expedition, this time to K2. Finding that permission to try his chosen objective had already been granted to the Italians, Herrligkoffer decided to try Gasherbrum I from the Siachen Glacier. He was granted permission by the Pakistani government, but the expedition's departure was delayed due to Herrligkoffer's commitments in Germany. Rather than allow the expedition to proceed without him, or to delay until 1955, Herrligkoffer decided upon a late summer/early autumn attempt. The expedition was then further delayed by problems with the Balti porters. Realising that his chances on Gasherbrum I were diminishing, Herrligkoffer changed objective, deciding instead to attempt Broad Peak, a mountain which had the advantage of being much closer to Concordia. As it was also an 8000m peak an ascent of Broad Peak would still be a considerable achievement. Herrligkoffer's team included three from Nanga Parbat, one being Kuno Rainer, Hermann Buhl's one-time climbing partner.

It was October 1954 before the expedition reached Concordia. From there Ernst Senn reconnoitred the Western Spur suggested by Dyhrenfurth and concluded that he had been correct: though clearly feasible it was too steep for the porters, passable only if it was strung with fixed ropes, a procedure which would take too long and, given the problems already encountered with the Baltis, one not in any event guaranteed to succeed. When Senn's view was confirmed by Toni Messner, Herrligkoffer transferred his interest to the southern side of the peak. On that side, the Broad Glacier opens into a glacial hollow between a long north–south ridge and the south-west ridge. Senn and Messner reported that this route looked more promising for the porters as it was less steep. The route also had the advantage of leading directly to the snowfield below the Wind Gap (as the 1957 Austrian team called what is now more usually termed Broad Col – the col between Broad Peak's main and central summits), but the disadvantage of appearing prone to avalanches. However, Messner noted that in the days they had spent investigating the route and its approaches they had actually not seen a large avalanche so that if the weather held the route might be fairly safe. On that far from optimistic note the climb began.

The plan was to establish camps at 5300m, 6000m, 6500m and 7200m, that last one set below the Wind Gap. The summit attempt would be made from there: it would seem that the team believed that what would later become known as the Forepeak was the true summit. The route turned out to be just as dangerous as Senn and Messner had feared, one 300m channel being known as the *Kanonenrohr*, the Cannon Barrel, for the way it channelled avalanches from a hanging glacier on the peak's west face down the route. Above this channel the route threaded a way through a maze of crevasses to reach a high plateau from where easy climbing reached a prominent triangular rock which the team called the *Eiskapelle* (Ice Chapel). Above this a steep (40°–50°) rock and ice wall ascended towards the snowfield below the Wind Gap. This had to be climbed on its left side as the right formed the upper edge of the Cannon Barrel. Climbing the wall proved hard, Ernst Senn claiming that it was as hard as anything he had encountered on the Matterhorn's

From Karl Herrligkoffer's book on the 1954 Austro-German Broad Peak expedition (Deutsche am Broad Peak). Herrligkoffer's team took a route on the south side of the mountain. The 1957 expedition linked to this route at around 6500m.

north face. At 7200m Senn and his climbing partner Michl Anderl reached a knee in the ridge. Beyond, easy ground led to the ice field below the Wind Gap, the col itself and the summit. The worst of the difficulties seemed behind them, but it was now 6 November and plunging temperatures and increasing storms meant the end of the expedition.

The team retreated: several climbers received minor injuries in major events – Senn fell 300m, but sustained only superficial injuries as the fall (more of a slide than a drop) ended in soft snow, and Sepp Maag and Rudl Marek fell into a crevasse and were lucky to escape with cuts and bruises – but everyone reached Concordia safely.

In the aftermath of the expedition Herrligkoffer wrote a book in which he noted that although the team had returned without reaching the summit, the expedition had 'led to an exemplary sense of comradeship that even now back home binds us togeth-

Taken in 1957, showing the same section of the mountain as for that on page 22. The Austrians followed (approximately) the 1954 route to the top of the conspicuous rib, then went left to reach Broad Col.

er far more fondly than the successful Nanga Parbat expedition in 1953 whose success was diminished by the zeal of individuals. If I had to choose between the two I would always go for the collaborative expedition that didn't reach the summit.' The sentiments are praiseworthy, but though apparently heart-felt they could not be expressed without a snipe at the Nanga Parbat expedition. Herrligkoffer's future as an expedition leader was also to show that he and controversy were almost constant companions.

2
The Dream

At the 40th anniversary of the Broad Peak climb the Austrian writer Helma Schimke made a short speech. Ms Schimke was herself a fine climber and had been present when Hermann Buhl and Marcus Schmuck, the two great climbers of the German-speaking world, had met for the first time at the Gaudeamus hut. She recalled that it was an extraordinary event, 'like a summer thunderstorm', the two men, each known to the other by reputation, metaphorically prowling around each other like stags weighing up an opponent before a territorial battle. When they finally spoke the conversation was filled with the names of great climbs, and also with the understatement that a climber will often fall into when cautiously sounding out another. I recall Schmuck telling me that at that first meeting Buhl had asked him how he had found one of his (Buhl's) new routes on the Maukspitze. Schmuck replied simply 'I did it', a response that climbers will recognise and understand. Helma Schimke went on to say that even at that first meeting it was clear that the two men had the greatest respect for each other and that from any friendship between them great things would develop. She had not been surprised that they had pushed back the frontiers of climbing: these two men, she claimed, particularly with their Broad Peak climb, would point the direction of climbing for the next 100 years.

Of the pair Hermann Buhl, by seven months the older of the

The Broad Peak team. Clockwise from top left: Marcus Schmuck, Hermann Buhl, Fritz Wintersteller and Kurt Diemberger. In the centre is Qader Saeed.

two, was by far the more famous. Indeed, at the time of that first meeting he was one of the most famous climbers in the world. Non-climbers of the period knew the names Hillary and Tenzing: if they knew another name at all it would be Hermann Buhl. In those days before mass travel the climbing world was largely a parochial one. The British might talk of Brown and Whillans, the Americans of Salathé and Schoening. The mountainous ridge of continental Europe linked France to Italy by way of Austria and Germany allowing easier movement, but it was still divided into western Alps, eastern Alps and Dolomites. The Italians spoke of Cassin and Bonatti, the French of Rebuffat and Terray. But climbers of every nation also spoke of Hermann Buhl.

Buhl had made early ascents of five of the six 'great north faces' of the Alps, his climbs including an outrageous solo of the north-east face of Piz Badile in four and a half hours, a performance which had required a mind shift in other climbers. The awe in which they had held the climb now became the awe in which they held the climber. Buhl had made an early ascent of the Eiger's north face, at that time the most feared and coveted climb in the world, in appalling weather, leading three ropes, combined out of necessity, to safety in a manner which drew admiration from Gaston Rebuffat who was leading one of the other ropes. And, of course, Hermann Buhl had climbed Nanga Parbat.

Marcus Schmuck's CV of famous climbs could not compare with Buhl's. Schmuck was a traveller as well as a climber. He had explored the Moroccan Sahara and the Atlas Mountains and made a remarkable journey on Spitsbergen, making first ascents of more than two dozen peaks, at a time when travel, and especially travel to such exotic locations, was unusual. On the rock of the ranges of the Austrian Alps around Salzburg he had put up great routes and carved a name for himself as the best of local rock climbers. On the east face of the Fleischbank in the Wilder Kaiser he had climbed a route which took a smooth, overhanging chimney. Hermann Buhl had attempted this, but called it a blind alley. Buhl was unable to get any pegs in for protection and eventually came to a halt. He claimed that at that point a hold broke. Buhl fell 50m, stopping on a ledge after his second's belay peg had been ripped. There were (and are) those who dispute the broken hold claim. What was certainly true was that the chimney had almost cost Buhl his life. Marcus Schmuck climbed it: it was graded VI+ and is still called the Schmuckkamin.

Schmuck had completed early ascents of many of Austria's finest climbs (including one or two by Buhl), but his list of routes included few in the western Alps, the major exception being an ascent of the Badile's north-east face in 1953, the year after Buhl's phenomenal solo climb. Like Buhl Schmuck had a young family. But unlike Buhl he did not have an employer who was understanding and forgiving, nor one who found Schmuck's reputation as a climber useful. Buhl helped out in shops selling climbing equipment, Marcus Schmuck was an electrician. He had to store up time off for his travelling and so was far more limited when it came to climbing away from the ranges near his Salzburg home. He had camped below some of the great climbs of the western Alps, but if the weather turned sour time would run out forcing him to abandon the attempt and return home.

After that first meeting which had so fired Helma Schimke, Buhl and Schmuck became climbing partners and friends. Schmuck readily admits that Buhl was better than he at climbing walls, but says he was the superior climber when it came to chimneys and corners. The combination of these abilities created a formidable team. Though it was a partnership of equals Schmuck was always impressed by Buhl's ability on blank walls. But much more than that he was impressed by Buhl's single-mindedness, by his ability to blank out everything that was not required in order to make progress up the route. Schmuck noted that when climbing with Buhl it was necessary to eat beforehand or to take snacks as Buhl forgot about the need to eat just as he dismissed everything else except the route. Schmuck also noted that the pleasure Buhl derived from a climb increased if the hardships increased. Bad weather, loose rock, all those things that other climbers found diminished their enthusiasm and pleasure, seemed merely to enhance Buhl's. This apparent masochism seems to have actually been another facet of Buhl's competitiveness. This is hardly the forum for a digression into psychology especially as any attempt would be at best amateur, but many have noted that Buhl's childhood – his mother died when he was four and he was placed in an orphanage, then shunned by his stepmother and, consequently, abandoned (at least partially) by his father – created an insecure youth who found emotional stability in the mountains and was driven to compete both with others and himself. Rather than use his remarkable talents to produce a string of new routes, Buhl more often felt the need to climb existing routes faster than his predecessors, or to do them in better style or worse conditions. This overt competitiveness comes across in his writing with its put-downs and side swipes – 'Couzy and Schatz (both first rate French climbers) rated the traverse VI, so it must be difficult. It's soon done, and I've done much harder traverses.' Not just 'harder' but 'much harder'. It is difficult not at least to consider the idea that on Nanga Parbat Hermann Buhl was secretly pleased when Otto Kempter, who was to have been his climbing partner on the summit attempt, failed to get past the Silver Saddle and so left the summit to Buhl alone.

In Marcus Schmuck, Buhl found a climber who could, more or less, match both his ability and his dedication. In 1956 the pair made an early repeat of the French route on the west face of the Petit Dru in record time as well as important early ascents of routes in the eastern Alps (for example the second ascent of the south-east arête on the Bischofsmütze in the Dachstein; a new start to the direct north face route on the same peak; and an ascent of the Laliderer north corner). Yet while they became one of the most effective partnerships at work in the Alps at the time, Buhl and Schmuck remained quite different. Hermann Buhl though married and with a young family – three daughters under the age of six at the time of his death – was a climber. Marcus Schmuck who had two sons and a daughter of similar ages to Buhl's was a family man and an electrician who climbed.

During their climbs in 1956 the two men would have discussed the expedition they planned making to the Karakoram in 1957. The perceived wisdom is that the idea of climbing Broad Peak was Buhl's, its concept his bequest to the climbing world. That idea fits neatly with the Buhl legend, but it does not fit with the facts.

It is undoubtedly true that after Nanga Parbat Buhl wished to return to the high hills, and particularly to the Karakoram. It is a point he makes early in the first report he sent home from Broad Peak: 'When I last saw the Nanga Parbat I secretly hoped to be able to gaze upon that mountain once again. The thought would not leave me alone. I seized upon the idea of a new expedition to the Karakorum [sic] – perhaps the Mustagh Tower, but the French and English beat me to it! They were quicker – or were they just better organisers?'

Buhl's desire to return was understandable, he was a top climber wishing to test himself once more against the tallest peaks. But the Nanga Parbat expedition had also left a legacy of another kind. It is not necessary to be either pro-Buhl or anti-Herrligkoffer to see the latter's behaviour after Nanga Parbat as unsympathetic at best, shameful at worst. It is clear that Buhl's extraordinary climb had saved Herrligkoffer's face, making a success of an expedition doomed to fail. Herrligkoffer's attempt to portray the climb as a team effort with Buhl merely a cog in a well-oiled machine was both at odds with reality and an affront to Buhl. Each man was striving to gain as much as possible from the climb. Herrligkoffer wanted to become a climbing entrepreneur, a man who could control the destiny of climbs and climbers. Buhl wanted to be the best and to be recognised as such. Ironically each man fulfilled his desires: Herrligkoffer led many more Himalayan expeditions, though often they became mired in controversy (most particularly another Nanga Parbat climb which saw the first climb of the vast Rupal face, but also the death of Günther Messner and the decision by Reinhold Messner to descend the other side of the mountain). Buhl found the fame he sought. In part he achieved that by breaking the contract Herrligkoffer had insisted each member of the Nanga

29

Parbat team sign before the expedition. The contract related to the use of material after the expedition. To part-finance the trip Herrligkoffer had sold the rights to the story of the expedition (in lectures, book form etc.) and needed to ensure that none of the climbers would do anything which might jeopardise this income. But Buhl's summit climb had gone ahead against the wishes of the leader and though it brought success Herrligkoffer was clearly upset by the 'mutiny' and, later, by the publicity the climb received. He portrayed the expedition as a group success, downplaying Buhl's role. Buhl resented this and, breaking the contract he had signed, published his own account of the climb and gave lectures on it. Many thought then, and still think now, that Buhl was justified in doing so because of Herrligkoffer's behaviour, but it is worth recalling that not everyone saw it that way.

After Nanga Parbat Buhl remained friends with Hans Ertl and Walter Frauenberger, who had met him at the top camp on his return from the summit (and had been part of the 'mutiny' against Herrligkoffer's directive to abandon the attempt). In 1955 Frauenberger was a member of the expedition which took Marcus Schmuck to Spitsbergen. On Spitsbergen Schmuck questioned Frauenberger about Nanga Parbat. As a traveller he wanted to see the Himalaya/Karakoram and as a climber he wanted to test his skills against the demands of the high hills. By inclination Schmuck preferred small expeditions comprised of friends: he was (and is) a cheerful, friendly man, better suited to small tight-knit groups than large, disparate teams. On Spitsbergen Schmuck began to think of organising a small team to attempt a big mountain, even at first suggesting to Frauenberger that the two of them should attempt it. The Austrian successes on Cho Oyu and Gasherbrum II had pointed the way. Marcus Schmuck began to think about the natural extension of these expeditions – do away with porters on the peak, transferring the Alpine approach to the high hills, and a plan began to form in his mind. Hermann Buhl was thinking along the same lines. He attempted to persuade his first climbing partner Luis Vigl and Luis' brother Hugo to join him on a trip, but they were too embedded in careers away from climbing for the idea to be practical. The meeting with Marcus Schmuck was a happy coincidence. Not only did the pair get on together but their skills and ambitions coincided. Helma Schimke's view that they would change the face of climbing over the next 100 years might have included an ambitious timescale, but was about to be proved right.

Marcus Schmuck claims that from his first thoughts in Spitsbergen his idea was to attempt Broad Peak. There is no reason to doubt that. Schmuck's ambition was for an 8000m peak. Of those unclimbed, Shisha Pangma was off-limits, Dhaulagiri had defeated several expeditions and was widely viewed at the time as being one of the most difficult of all the 8000m peaks (Lionel Terray, the great French climber, had declared it unclimbable in 1950, always a rash judgement, but not one to be dismissed lightly when voiced by such an authority), while Gasherbrum I was only a few metres higher than Broad Peak and had the disadvantage of being much more difficult to reach. If there were problems with the porters Schmuck would have to employ to reach base camp (as there often was in the Baltoro) then he would be stranded too far from his mountain.

Hermann Buhl may have favoured Broad Peak for the same reasons. But he had other reasons for wanting it. After the Nanga Parbat expedition Herrligkoffer was the chief target for Buhl's anger, but not the only one. Buhl also felt betrayed by other members of the team, not least Kuno Rainer. Rainer had been Buhl's partner in the years immediately prior to the expedition, their climbs including early repeats of the Walker Spur on the Grandes Jorasses and the Cassin route on Cima Ovest, and the first winter ascent of the south-west face of the Marmolada. Buhl and Rainer had been seen as a probable summit team, but Rainer's trip had not gone well, ill-health forcing him to stay low on the peak. After the expedition Rainer sided with the leader, a move widely seen as being a (successful) attempt to earn a place on Herrligkoffer's 1954 expedition. That had been to Broad Peak, and had been unsuccessful. It is not difficult to imagine the satisfaction that success on Broad Peak would have given Buhl had he ever met Herrligkoffer or Rainer again.

The Team

The two men applied for permission to climb Broad Peak naming Masherbrum as an alternative, as at the time there were often problems obtaining climbing permits from the Pakistani government and experience had shown that a willingness to compromise paid dividends. As Buhl was employed in a shop specialising in climbing equipment, and because he had high-altitude and Karakoram experience, he agreed to handle equipment. Schmuck, the more practical of the two, began detailed planning of the trip and also began to worry about finances. Financially the expedition would place an extreme burden on the two men. They expected to be away four months (a correct assessment – Marcus Schmuck left Salzburg on 29 March 1957 and arrived back on 26 July – though after Broad Peak had been climbed there was friction between the two men over exactly when they would return). Each man had a young family and was the sole breadwinner. Neither was of independent means. While Buhl, the famous climber, could reasonably expect to be able to pick up his job in a sports shop again on his return and to be in demand for lectures, Schmuck's position was more precarious. Though qualified as an electrician and therefore unlikely to be out of work for long, he was likely to be a less sought-after lecturer. Schmuck worked as long as he could, leaving his job one week before his departure. While he was away he continued to pay his Austrian social security dues so that he could be reinstated in his job when he returned. He began work again on 1 August, just six days after his return from the expedition.

For each family there were difficult and uncertain times ahead. If Schmuck had failed to return his wife would have returned to work, aided in bringing up the children by her in-laws. When Buhl failed to return his wife brought up a young family on her own, her income dependent on the generosity of family and friends, and on the royalties from Buhl's Nanga Parbat book. During the expedition both families survived on their savings, Schmuck's wife and children benefiting from food packed into the family home's basement: the expedition had been unable to take everything which arrived and the surplus

The Austrians at the Sunhäusl (Sunhouse) Inn at Maria Alm, a village close to Salzburg, in early 1957. Marcus Schmuck was born in this village in 1925. From left to right are Schmuck, Buhl, Diemberger (with guitar),Wintersteller and an unknown man.

helped Frau Schmuck to feed her children.

Marcus Schmuck was also faced with another problem. He was chairman of the Salzburg section of the Alpenverein (the Austrian Alpine Association) and could reasonably have expected to obtain the organisation's enthusiastic support. He did not get it. The natural assumption that a revolutionary expedition involving the legendary Hermann Buhl would be supported proved false. Far from embracing the idea the Alpenverein (particularly the Innsbruck section of which Buhl was a member) agreed to support the plan only if Buhl did not go. He was too difficult, too controversial. The aftermath of Nanga Parbat, irrespective of the merits of the case on either side, had been unseemly. No one wanted another expedition that ended on the front pages of the newspapers or, worse, in the courts. It seems that the organisation was still smarting from Buhl's breaking of his contract over the repayment of money for the Nanga Parbat trip. The Austrian members of Herrligkoffer's expedition had apparently agreed to repay their costs to the Alpenverein. Buhl had not done this, taking the view that this contract was a part of the one with Herrligkoffer which he disputed.

But Schmuck insisted. He needed Buhl's high-altitude expertise, as well as his drive. Buhl was also his friend and after the talking and planning he would not let him down. In the end a compromise was reached. Marcus Schmuck, not Hermann Buhl, would be the leader of the expedition and the Alpenverein would offer support. There would be limited financial support, but, very importantly, they would allow their name to be used in the search for finance. The expedition would be the Austrian Alpenverein Karakoram Expedition 1957, leader Marcus Schmuck. This having been agreed, Schmuck and Buhl made an agreement that on the mountain Schmuck would surrender the leadership in deference to Buhl's experience. On 2 March 1957 the two formalised this position, signing an agreement produced by Buhl (a fact which led Schmuck to make a comment in the margin on how good a businessman Buhl was) which covered the leadership and other, unrelated, issues. Schmuck's other margin comments included the hope that the two men could make the Alpenverein accept the agreement. It was a forlorn hope.

Ultimately the Alpenverein contributed 60,000 Schillings (the final cost of the expedition was 205,000 Schillings) funded through contributions from various sections of the organisation. In a letter to Schmuck in December 1956 Buhl wrote: 'To be frank, I would never have dreamt that the Alpenverein would be so supportive and to make such a generous contribution.' He was right to be stunned, but would have been less surprised by the knowledge that the Innsbruck section of the Alpenverein gave very little.

The agreement between the two men over the leadership, taken at face value, seems amicable, but there are good reasons to believe that Buhl was much more aggrieved than it appears. The decision that he should be 'leader on the mountain' is an indication of his enthusiasm to be leader. For Buhl the leadership of his own expedition was the logical step in his development as a climber and it seems that the fact that his view was not shared by others was a snub he felt keenly.

In the letter to Schmuck in which he mentioned the Alpenverein's donation Buhl also wrote that he had discussed finances with Fritz Moravec, the leader of the successful 1956 Gasherbrum II expedition, at a lecture Moravec had given on that climb. He was to meet him again – 'Tomorrow I am meeting Moravec and we will discuss all the important issues concerning travel, costs, the walk to Broad Peak etc. because he can give me good advice. He thinks the costs of the expedition would come to 50,000 Schillings per person which wouldn't be very high. However costs are likely to increase a bit because of the present difficulties concerning the travel route.' The difficulties that concerned Buhl were those likely to be caused by the Suez crisis. Buhl goes on to suggest to Schmuck that as well as the sources of cash he has already tried (Schmuck had by then raised 100,000 Schillings) he might consider the Austrian Ministry of Education and Sport, and the Sport-toto (the equivalent of the British football pools). Schmuck tried both and received a donation from each. He was less successful with another Buhl suggestion, that he try for reduced fares from shipping and airline companies.

During their early discussions it became clear to the two men that the quantity of equipment and food that would need to be carried to the base of the mountain would place a huge burden on them. As the amount of money Schmuck and Buhl (who was attempting to raise cash in Germany) gathered increased, it became clear that they could afford a third climber. Marcus Schmuck chose Fritz Wintersteller, a fellow resident of Salzburg, who had also been on the Spitsbergen expedition. Though less gifted than Buhl and Schmuck, Wintersteller, the youngest of the trio by three years, was a good climber. He had climbed grade VI routes before his sixteenth birthday and completed an early ascent of the Comici route on the north wall of the Cima Grande. But then a badly-broken leg had put a temporary stop to his fledgling career in the mountains. As well as climbing ability Wintersteller possessed what Schmuck termed a peculiar sense for finding the correct route or the right place for a camp. From their time in Spitsbergen, where the two had climbed several peaks together, Schmuck also knew that Wintersteller kept his head in the most trying situations, a fact which made him an ideal third member. Wintersteller was also immensely strong – and still is, defying his age with skiing, swimming and cycling feats that would tax someone young enough to be his grandchild. He came from a family known collectively as 'the bulls' for their strength and stamina. Like Schmuck, Wintersteller was an electrician. He was also, as the expedition was to discover, a brilliant odd-job man. To maintain his large frame Fritz Wintersteller ate a lot. He also enjoyed cooking and, unsurprisingly, was given the task of organising the expedition's food when he accepted the invitation to join.

The correspondence between Schmuck and Buhl reveals the care with which they prepared the trip, a methodical approach that belies the sense of excitement both felt as 1956 drew to a close. In a letter of early December 1956 written from Sporthaus Scheck in Munich where he was then employed, Buhl presented his apologies for not meeting Schmuck in Innsbruck, then explained that he had been able to persuade the owner of the shop not only to allow him the time to take part in the expedition, but also to provide the equipment they needed in exchange for being the sole equipment provider and therefore having the sole rights to trade on that fact. Buhl showed that his view of sponsorship was a very modern one by noting that this 'shouldn't bother us because it doesn't matter whoever does it. If you ask for something you have to give something in return. At least we will know that getting the equipment is in safe hands and also that the climb will be promoted while we are away so that when we come back the public will already be aware of it.' Buhl expands on this view in his expedition reports: 'We don't want things for nothing. In exchange we offer wonderful pictures, assessments of products, reports, advertising – advertising is everything these days.' A thoroughly modern attitude. Buhl's attitude to public awareness was also surprisingly modern. Such awareness would clearly be of benefit for the intended lecture tour.

After this good news Buhl's letter raised three issues which bothered him. The first issue was raised only obliquely. Buhl said that he had had to approach the owner of Sporthaus Scheck in part because 'I have already worked out a plan for some hard climbs until May or June that only I can carry out.' Although everything was going ahead on the assumption that Buhl would be going, Schmuck had not yet successfully concluded his negotiations with the Alpenverein over this. Buhl had therefore to consider the possibility that the expedition would depart without him, and, indeed, the possibility that it would not depart at all because permission had not yet at that stage been granted. As an aside, Buhl's competitiveness is yet again evident in his words: 'hard climbs … which only I can carry out.' And this in a letter to a friend and climbing partner.

The second issue was much more directly raised. It was Herrligkoffer. Buhl wrote 'Herrligkoffer, now that the news has

The team looking somewhat out-of-place in formal clothing at a reception at which Governor Klaus of Salzburg (who later became the Austrian Chancellor) wished them bon voyage a few days before Diemberger and Wintersteller departed. From the left: Schmuck, Diemberger, Buhl and Wintersteller.

got out, will try anything to beat us to it and we have to prevent that. He has very good relations with Bonn, the German consul in Pakistan, and the Pakistani authorities, and Germany is particularly influential in Pakistan.' The third issue was health: 'I am repeatedly asked if we are taking a doctor on the expedition. We need to consider this and I'd like your opinion. I am still in favour of going with a team of three, but the argument for taking a doctor cannot be dismissed easily.'

Buhl's concerns over a doctor are understandable. In his account of the aftermath of the Nanga Parbat climb he compared his return from the peak with that of Maurice Herzog from Annapurna, noting that despite his much worse injuries Herzog at least had friends and a good doctor with him. Pointedly he noted that 'there was no Dr Oudot among my team mates.' Though this was clearly a snipe at Herrligkoffer, Buhl knew first-hand the consequences of a lack of medical competence in the Karakoram. At the time the Broad Peak team had no money for a doctor, even if a willing one could be found, but so good were Marcus Schmuck's fund-raising efforts that ultimately a fourth member could be afforded. But then Schmuck baulked at taking a doctor. He felt that a fourth climber was what was needed and that climbing ability should be the only criterion for choosing. His preferred candidate was Rudolf Bardodej, his rope mate during the early years of his climbing career, but it was not to be. Before any approaches could be made the Viennese section of the Alpenverein put pressure on the Salzburg section to include a different man.

Kurt Maix was president of the Viennese section. He was a writer as well as a climber, and had been the collaborator/editor of Hermann Buhl's book. Maix was an admirer of Buhl (when asked once what proof there was that Buhl had reached the summit of Nanga Parbat Maix replied 'He came back didn't he?', a formidable response), and was now also an admirer of another young climber – Kurt Diemberger. As well as putting pressure on Salzburg, Maix recommended Diemberger to Buhl. Diemberger's credentials were good despite his age – he was 26 ('alarmingly young' as Buhl notes in one of his reports). Diemberger had made an early ascent of the Matterhorn's north face and was credited with the ascent of a curious mushroom-like ice structure at the summit of the Königsspitze. The Mushroom, into which a battle station had been burrowed during the 'White War' of the 1914–18 conflict, was only climbed once more after Diemberger's ascent, the whole structure then collapsing. The Viennese recommended Diemberger as the fourth member of the team with the suggestion that he was the best ice climber in Austria, a claim which gave the existing three team members a much needed laugh in the serious business of preparing the expedition. Wintersteller now claims that even at the time doubts were circulating about Diemberger's Mushroom climb and that he, Buhl and Schmuck were suspicious of it. Today the two climbers who were with Diemberger on the day (in particular Dr Herbert Knapp who has spoken at length with the author about the climb) still dispute Diemberger's version of events. But Buhl, Schmuck and Diemberger were unable to decline the Viennese suggestion – and had no real reason to do so, none of them had met Diemberger at that time – so the trio pressed him into service as team doctor. Anxious to get to the high hills, Diemberger was not in a position to decline this offer and became the team's nominal doctor.

It would be anticipated that the four members of the expedition were now eager to be on their way and that when, in early March, half the team and all the equipment left for Pakistan, all outstanding issues had been resolved. But the latter was not the case. After the departure of Diemberger and Wintersteller problems between Buhl and the Alpenverein flared up again.

On hearing of the agreement between Schmuck and Buhl the Alpenverein decided that a formal, and comprehensive, contract was required, and drew one up for the two men to sign. Schmuck signed on 24 March, but Buhl declined to add his signature. Departure for the two men was just five days away. Buhl's refusal to sign was not helped by events at an Alpenverein meeting in Graz where the organisation's General-Secretary, Dr Schmied-Wallenburg, made some clearly heartfelt, but injudicious, comments. He noted that after Nanga Parbat

Buhl had demanded an apartment for his family from the Alpenverein on the grounds that his status merited it. He wanted the Alpenverein to pay the rent and to provide other favours, and when the organisation refused Buhl resigned. He rejoined only when the Broad Peak expedition was discussed, a move seen by the Alpenverein as calculated to force their hand over leadership of the expedition. Schmied-Wallenburg noted that the Alpenverein had refused Buhl the leadership: he was a prima donna and did not have the character to represent Austria abroad. Indeed, Schmied-Wallenburg said, the Alpenverein were planning to hold an inquiry into Buhl's behaviour as despite having been refused the leadership he had recently given interviews in which he had said he was the leader. Schmied-Wallenburg's remarks were reported in the *Neuer Kurier* newspaper on 25 March.

Buhl's refusal to sign the contract – and, doubtless the reported remarks – brought other newspapers into the argument. Vienna's *Bild Telegraf* ran a headline – Why won't Buhl sign? – above an article which noted that Diemberger and Wintersteller were now in the Indian Ocean unaware that a crisis was threatening the expedition. This time Schmied-Wallenburg was quoted as saying that he could not understand Buhl's position: the contract was no pact with the devil but a standard form other expeditions had willingly signed. His example was Tichy's team who had all signed a similar contract before Cho Oyu. The contract is indeed innocuous, dealing with the need for regular reports, lectures to be given on return, expedition accounts to be prepared etc. but there were two problems with it. The first was that it tied Buhl to timescales for publishing his own account of the climb which, coupled with Buhl's suspicions of contracts in general after his Herrligkoffer experience, was enough to bother him. The second was that the contract could be read as denying Sporthaus Scheck access to photographs for up to 12 months after the team returned, and left ambiguous the final ownership of Scheck's equipment. As Otto Scheck was putting up both equipment and cash he was not happy. And Buhl worked for Scheck.

On 24 March, the day Schmuck signed, the Alpenverein sent an ultimatum to Buhl by telegram telling him to sign by 8pm on 25 March or he could not join the expedition, causing Buhl to employ a lawyer who telegrammed back saying that his client (Buhl) was happy with the Schmuck-Buhl agreement, but not with the new contract. It looked like an impasse, and an internal Alpenverein memo considered what the organisation's position would be if Buhl continued to refuse: in that event steps would be taken to ensure he did not board the aircraft; if he managed to reach Pakistan, Schmuck would be told to give him his equipment and send him away. Finally, at a meeting which involved the Governor of Salzburg (the problems now having become a national issue) and Otto Scheck himself, a resolution was found. Quite what the resolution was is not obvious. Whether Buhl actually signed the contract is unclear: the copy in the Alpenverein archives has only Schmuck's signature. But, of course, Buhl's death made everything irrelevant.

The contract problems were clearly stressful, but was there more? In conversation with Horst Höfler, Louis Vigl (Buhl's early climbing partner, now sadly deceased) said that as the time for departure drew close Buhl's health was giving his friends cause for concern. Buhl was very depressed over the leadership issue, and physically exhausted by the effort of fundraising and the organising of equipment. Vigl maintained that the leadership was the real issue, but the contract (which does not mention it) could not have helped. Vigl said that Buhl's health was such that another friend had become so concerned for Buhl's well-being that he had even once suggested that he wished he could break Buhl's arm or leg in order to prevent him from travelling. These reports are given credence by entries in the first of Buhl's typed reports from the expedition where he notes: 'I was still counting on a short period for recuperation, for the mad rush gnaws away at our nerves more and more from one day to the next and creates the worst conditions for an expedition. But then the farewells follow …' and, later, 'As for my planned skiing holiday with my wife, which I wanted to make before my departure, both for my health and for her sake, nothing much came of it.'

3
The Expedition

Diemberger and Wintersteller, the youngest and both unmarried, were sent ahead, by ship with the 1800kg of equipment and food the expedition needed. The Suez Crisis had forced closure of the canal to all shipping which meant that the two men had to travel around Africa. They left Salzburg by train on 3 March 1957 after a farewell ceremony hosted by the city's mayor and embarked on the *Asia*, a 10,000ton passenger ship, from Genoa on 6 March. Diemberger says that the two jogged around the ship's deck thirty times daily to maintain fitness. Wintersteller's version differs, noting that he (Wintersteller) did much more jogging, especially at night when Diemberger was keener on the attention being paid to him by another passenger, a pretty Japanese girl. Wintersteller also had a nightly routine of deep knee bends, raising his body weight on one leg at a time, and repeating the exercise 100 times per leg. He had calculated that leg strength was likely to be the key to success on Broad Peak: he was to be proved right, and the regime was to play an important part in the eventual success on the mountain. The effect of the fitness regime on the two young men can be seen in times quoted in Wintersteller's diary:

07/03   Thursday, Naples 09:10, Vesuvius 10:00. To peak 13:00.
20/03   Wednesday, Cape Town 08:00. Bus from harbour. 09:00 to Kloofnek 10:00. To peak 12:30. Funicular from Table Mountain 13:00. Bus to harbour 15:00.

Base Camp, dominated by the beautiful southern side of K2.

The telegram which gave the Austrians permission to attempt Broad Peak. The telegram was sent on 26 March, three weeks after the ship carrying Diemberger, Wintersteller and the expedition's equipment had left Genoa.

The voyage seems to have been pleasant and relaxing. Although Diemberger and Wintersteller never became close, they got on well enough. At one point, Diemberger says, the two toasted Nasser and his decision to close the Suez Canal, offering them the journey of a lifetime with time spent in Dakar and Mogadishu as well as Cape Town. Diemberger's reaction was very different from that expressed by Hermann Buhl in his Christmas letter to Marcus Schmuck in which he had been concerned that the crisis over the canal might actually stop the expedition completely or, at least, increase the costs considerably. On 3 April the *Asia* reached Karachi where the team was reunited.

The journey of Buhl and Schmuck to Karachi was a far less relaxing affair. The pair flew to Pakistan, Schmuck leaving Salzburg on 29 March intending to join Buhl at Munich. Schmuck's description of his departure, with his children tying him to a chair at home during the midday meal, is a reminder of similar leavings for all who travel away from their families, and one that is all the more poignant when it is remembered that Hermann Buhl's children were, unknowingly, also saying sad

44

and fond farewells to a father who would not be coming home. As Buhl notes: 'The atmosphere at the airport is suited to a reunion but not to a farewell, especially for a Himalaya expedition. One is separated too quickly, the last minutes unfortunately spent at customs and with the usual bureaucracy.'

Schmuck's 82-year-old father was at Salzburg Airport, perplexed and shaking his head at this curious decision of his son to leave his family and cross the world to climb a mountain. Family members then accompanied Schmuck to the plane, a memory of a time before security dominated the air corridors. The flight was operated by KLM, which required a roundabout route, Schmuck travelling to Munich, then Amsterdam, then, the next day, to Rome. It was only in Rome that Buhl finally joined the flight, Schmuck having been greeted at Munich by Buhl still dragging luggage into the airport and saying that he needed one more day to finish the job. There were also reporters from local newspapers who, despite Schmuck's attempts to drag all conversations back to Broad Peak, wanted only to discuss the problems between the Alpenverein and Buhl over the contract and the expedition leadership.

As another reminder of the (relatively) early days of passenger aviation, the plane was a Convair CEG 240 which went no higher than 2730m on its way to Amsterdam. Next day Schmuck was in a Super-Constellation en route for Düsseldorf, Zürich and Rome. During the flight he caught sight of the Matterhorn and Monte Rosa, recalling his ascent of the latter's east face, the snow made treacherous by a warm night. In Rome Buhl joined the flight which continued through the night to Beirut. After a short stop the plane flew on towards Karachi, but very soon the two men were alarmed by a severe rocking. An engine had failed and the flight was forced to return to Beirut, the pilot jettisoning fuel to stop the plane from losing height. For Buhl the sight was '... a bit spooky ... I still remember from the war the smoke trails of planes that had been shot down', a reminder that both he and Schmuck had been conscripted into the German army during the last phase of the 1939–45 war. Buhl had been captured in Italy, Schmuck was wounded and captured in Normandy.

It seems from Schmuck's description that the passengers were lucky the failure was so soon after take-off. The pilot had to make constant adjustments to keep the plane airborne long enough to return to the airport: had they been several hours into the flight and far from an emergency runway the pilot's task might have been more difficult. For his part Buhl was convinced the aircraft would not make it. The pilot had taken it on a long circle back to Beirut and so approached the city from over the sea. Buhl could see the white horses on the water and was 'already preparing myself for a bath' when land appeared.

The delay offered the pair the chance of a good night's rest in a classy hotel and a trip to Baalbeck to see the ancient temples. Buhl was impressed by both the drive to Baalbeck and the site itself. On the way he noted that 'peasants still till the soil with wooden ploughs' and gives a description of the ruins which suggests either great interest and a good memory or the purchase of a guide book. He ends his description by noting that he left Baalbeck '… respectfully … (a place) of so much history, where so much blood and sweat was shed.'

On 2 April the flight continued to Karachi without incident. Buhl's description of dawn seen from the plane is an indication of his growing prowess as a writer – 'The eastern horizon offers a true symphony of colour. The sky is still black, but the horizon starts to glow red, the red becoming ever deeper, then fading into light ochre, becoming a light blue and then turning into the black of space. A painter couldn't do it any better. Between the fluffy clouds I can see the black of the Persian Gulf. The plane is bathed in pink light and then it seems as if it has been drowned in blood, the rotating propeller looking like a glowing wheel of fire. The clouds beneath us put on their morning dress and like the golden points of lances the first beams of the rising fire-ball stab into the bloody mass of the wings.'

At Karachi Buhl and Schmuck were met by an official from the Austrian Embassy, taken to their hotel and then to the Embassy for lunch. At the Embassy the two men were able to thank the Austrian Ambassador, Dr Fritz Hartlmayr, whose personal intervention was significant in obtaining permission for Broad Peak. The satisfaction with which Buhl must have received the news that permission had been granted to the team rather than to Herrligkoffer can be imagined. What is certain is that Buhl was recalling his last visit to the city when 'with my frostbitten foot I limped up the stairs not knowing if I would ever return. I could only hope.'

The following day the two men headed for the harbour to meet the *Asia*, and spent time dragging Diemberger away from the Japanese girl. That evening the team were invited to dinner at the Austrian Embassy where, it seems, the entire Austrian population of Pakistan had gathered to wish them well. After the meal there was talk of home, as might be expected, and then Buhl and Diemberger entertained the assembly by singing Austrian folk songs, a much less expected event. This small nugget of information allows an altogether different light to fall on Buhl whose usual image is that of uncompromising hard man of the hills.

The epic flights of Schmuck and Buhl then continued. Having put the equipment, Diemberger and Wintersteller on the train for Lahore, the two older men flew there, uneventfully, Schmuck having time to admire both the stewardesses and the scenery below. In a lyrical passage from his expedition diary Schmuck reveals a man of sensitivity, intensely interested in his surroundings, and a man with a gift for expressing this interest. The flight then continued to Rawalpindi, but after half an hour hit a thunderstorm. The plane was thrown about violently, the food and water which was to have been served to the passengers being flung through the cabin. Schmuck recalls being jolted around despite his seatbelt, watching lightning flashing across the sky outside and pandemonium inside with frightened, frantic passengers being comforted by the stewardesses. So bad did the lurching and shaking become that Schmuck – who, sat at the back, could see the whole cabin flexing as the shock waves hit it – seriously wondered if the plane would survive. Eventually the pilot escaped the thunder, but returned to Lahore rather than risk hitting it again. Back at their hotel Buhl retired early with diarrhoea and a fever. His illness was a prelude to the stomach problems which apparently plagued him throughout the expedition.

Camp between Askole and Paiju during the walk-in.

On 6 April Buhl and Schmuck had a more peaceful flight to Rawalpindi, meeting the other two there. In the afternoon Schmuck, accompanied by Diemberger, acquired permission for the team to fly to Skardu (this was a time of increased tensions with India over Kashmir – half a century on and things have not improved – and so Pakistan was understandably cautious of foreign travellers) and began organising porters for the trek along the Baltoro. The next day the team rested, but in the way that climbing expeditions do. Wintersteller claimed he was willing to do anything except climb the big willow tree in front of the hotel which led, inevitably, to a competition. Schmuck also visited the local bazaar where 'craftsmen sit in the huts producing their wares, women with children and beggars are everywhere … though flies form the majority of the population.' The Austrians 'can never stay still because if we stop we are immediately surrounded by curious people.'

At Rawalpindi the team met Qader Saeed, their liaison officer. The 24-year old Qader had been born in southern India, his family moving to Pakistan after the partition which followed the granting of independence to British India. The Austrians were told that there was no chance of a flight before 12 April, which was lucky for Schmuck as he had now gone down with a severe attack of diarrhoea which kept him in the hotel for two days while Diemberger took care of changing the money for paying the porters. Perhaps recalling that on the British Everest expedition it had taken twelve porters to carry the boxes of coins required to pay all the porters, Schmuck was very grateful that in Pakistan the locals were willing to take paper money. The whole team then went on an exquisite two-day trip which so entranced the now-recovered Schmuck that in his diary he has to use single word shorthand so that his writing can keep up with the memories flowing through his head. The first day was through a landscape of 'river, mountains visible, blocks of granite, little donkeys, veiled women. The land of Swat. Wonderful mosque, many children, bazaar in sunset. Persian script! Little shops – baker, shoemaker, tailor, inns. Stay overnight at Swat hotel – children with beautiful faces, girls with nose rings, evening table tennis with locals, 24.00 bed.'

The second day was just as good: '7000m background, presumably Tirich Mir, a grave with prayer flags, high, green valleys. Pass, beautiful road – Kabul river – raft bridge – Peshawar. Large market, water buffalo, carts, great alleys. Travel on through desert-like areas – caravans of camels, nomads' tents, many colourful people. Passport control, hand over camera: photos not allowed. Caves in the mountain for accommodation, mountain roads to the Khyber Pass wonderfully built, two roads: car and caravans, street signs with pictures because most are illiterate, beautiful rail tracks, vultures, sinuous descent towards Afghanistan.'

Buhl also enjoyed the trips, noting that on the first day the way the Austrians attracted local children made him feel like the Pied Piper. On the second day Buhl drove the party back to Rawalpindi – 'Delightful drive, three hours from Peshawar… about 50–60 miles per hour.' Buhl is obviously giving the speed from the resolutely British speedometer of the hire car.

The Austrians returned to Rawalpindi to be ready for their flight but despite near perfect conditions they were told that the weather at Skardu was bad. On 13 April, with conditions in Rawalpindi far worse, the team made their way pessimistically to the airport only to discover that the flight was on. Buhl had hoped to be able to see Nanga Parbat on the flight but it was hidden by cloud.

At Skardu, while they were waiting for the arrival of porters from Askole (chosen because they had heard that porters from there were more reliable than those from Skardu), Schmuck and Wintersteller, the two electricians, discussed with the local Political Agent the possibility of building a 5MW power station for the locals. The project is a recurrent theme throughout the diaries of both men, but never came to fruition.

The last days and nights before the expedition began in earnest seem to have been a time of nostalgia. On Palm Sunday (14 April) Schmuck writes that Hermann Buhl was the 'Palm Sunday Donkey', a Pinzgau expression for the last of a party to get up on that particular day. Then there was a meal with the Political Agent at which Diemberger played guitar as the others sang songs tinged with sadness, and finally Schmuck's diary notes that Hermann Buhl played the guitar beneath a dark sky with the moonlight illuminating the peaks of the Karakoram far away, adding that despite the homesickness the team 'are happy with our fate.' The following day Schmuck wrote that if you are sitting in the courtyard of a comfortable inn, a wooden board for a writing desk, with, in front of you, an apricot tree in blossom and, beyond, snow-covered peaks against a marvellously blue sky it is difficult not to be a poet. But it is also not easy to forget that you are far from home and that the future holds unknown risks. Buhl's diary makes no mention of the homesickness, only that he shaves for the last time. (Later in a note to his wife attached to one of his reports Buhl tells her that the four have all grown proper beards and that 'mine is naturally the wildest'.)

The porters arrived on 18 April, Marcus Schmuck's 32nd birthday ('I've never been so far from home on my birthday, but

On the walk-in near Paiju.

I've never been 32 years old before either'), and the expedition left Skardu. The journey along the Baltoro is now so familiar that it seems redundant to follow the team's accounts. But it is instructive for two reasons, the first and most obvious being to highlight the differences between the route then and the route now. The second is to gain an insight into the development of the team. Before Skardu, apart from the sea voyage of Kurt Diemberger and Fritz Wintersteller, the men had spent little time together (though Buhl and Schmuck, and Schmuck and Wintersteller had been climbing partners prior to the trip). Now, finally, the team were together and the idiosyncrasies that could make and break friendships were to become apparent.

To Concordia

The Austrians were up by 6am, Schmuck and Wintersteller organising the 65 porters for a trek which started with a crossing of the Indus. Schmuck was the last to leave the Skardu base and it is not difficult to imagine this poetic man taking a last look around and wondering about the circumstances under which he would see it again, particularly as the Political Agent and other dignitaries had come to wish them a safe return, knowing that some who had made the journey had not returned. The ferryman was paid 12 rupees and needed to make three trips to get everyone across the river. The trek then crossed burning sand, Wintersteller noting that his pulse (usually 45) rose to over 100 in the strong sun and thinning air. He also noted that someone complained of a headache, another of sunburnt thighs. The Austrians had employed porters from both Askole and Satpura, and the rivalry between the two groups meant that the four men frequently had to ask the porters to take it easy and were happy to reach a tiny oasis with a clear stream where rest and chapattis allowed a respite from the effort. At 2.30pm the expedition reached the Shigar oasis with its blossoming apricot trees, mulberries and poplars. They camped on the polo field, Buhl and Diemberger singing again as they erected the tents, and ate a meal of local produce – chicken, eggs and chapattis – so as to conserve their European food. At 8pm they made for their sleeping bags, but despite the efforts of the day Schmuck did not sleep well. Excitement? Nervousness?

On Good Friday (19 April) the Austrians rose in the cold of the early morning and the expedition was underway again at 6.45am, the first three hours of the day's march being through apricot orchards in pleasant temperatures. Schmuck noted that white stones had been placed, like little doves, to mark the path so that it could be followed even at night. Later, as they moved up the Shigar valley a sandstorm blew up coating everything with a fine layer of dust and penetrating the team's cameras as well as their noses and mouths. The strong wind forced them to camp in an old riverbed near Koshumal where the only water was dubiously muddy. Wintersteller, who had already become close to the porters, was told of a well and headed off to get a better supply, though that, too, was grey and miserable looking. That night the team dined on chickens, eggs and chapattis again.

In his diary of the day's trek Schmuck wrote that he and Wintersteller, together with Qader had hurried on ahead during the sandstorm to find the camp site. That night he noted that Buhl and Diemberger were singing in the next tent, the first indication he gives that partnerships which would later re-appear on the mountain had been forged. It could be argued that as Buhl and Schmuck had travelled together, as had the younger men, a change of partner was understandable and it had been agreed at the outset that everyone would take a turn to climb with the legendary Buhl. But there was, as yet, no climbing and Buhl and Schmuck were friends. In conversation, Diemberger hinted at a darker possibility. He insists that Buhl's aggravation at the loss of the leadership of the expedition to Schmuck was the reason, the agreement with Schmuck over the transfer of leadership on the mountain being insufficient to sat-isfy Buhl's ego. Diemberger says, and many others agree, that Buhl was sensitive to criticism and perceived slights – 'as sensi-tive as a mimosa' is the expression Diemberger is fond of using. In voicing this opinion Diemberger adds further credence to Vigl's view that the leadership issue had depressed Buhl. Perhaps Buhl was already distancing himself from someone he considered a rival who had won the first exchange.

For the following day (20 April) Wintersteller's diary reveals just how close he had grown to the porters. Fritz is a mountain man, a man used to carrying big loads and making trail. He is also a man of action and was fascinated by everything about the porters' way of life. This day he walked ahead with a group of Askole porters led by Qasim Ali who had been with the Italian expedition to K2. Wintersteller watched intently as 'the Braldu comes into view and the porters stop at an oasis for their chap-atti pause. In very quick time they have made a fire using dry branches from bushes and prepared tea, which they improve with ghee (rancid butter) and a pinch of salt. Chapattis are then baked on heated stones. These and the tea are the porters' lunch.' Wintersteller also noted that 'this diet will soon also be ours – once we get used to it.' It was the salted butter tea which would take the most getting used to. Schmuck grabbed a cup before the ghee and salt went in, provoking laughter about the difference between 'sahib tea' and real tea. Buhl, arriving late, missed out on the 'sahib tea' and, his stomach still fragile, was revolted by the cup of real tea he was passed. After the tea and chapattis the porters smoked, some with water pipes they had brought, some by creating a pipe in the sand, forming a tube and filling it with tobacco, several taking turns to smoke the sand pipe, while others improvised a water pipe from a tin of Löwenbräu discarded by the Austrians the day before.

That night at Dassu, after the stream of porters carrying the expedition's aluminium chests and kitbags arrived, the team supplemented their now-usual diet of chicken and eggs (two chickens and 24 eggs between the four sahibs and Qader) with fresh apricots. After the sun had set, in the cool of twilight Schmuck listened to Buhl and Diemberger singing 'in their usual wonderful way.' Then, as night fell they heard strange, eerie sounds. They were the calls of the Mullah as it was Muharram (both Schmuck and Wintersteller claim in their diaries that it was Ramadan, but in conversation Qader Saeed assures me that Muharram is correct), the porters not being allowed to eat between sunrise and sunset (which makes one wonder about the daily chapatti stops). Both Schmuck and Wintersteller were reminded of the *Jedermann* in the Domplatz of their native Salzburg. (The Jedermann (Everyman) is a musical play constructed around the life and death of a rich man. Written by Hofmannsthal it was first performed in 1920 as the opening of the Salzburg Festival and is now an essential part of each year's event.) The association made Schmuck very homesick, reminding him that usually on Easter Saturday he was with his family planning how they would spend the following day. This night he was thousands of kilometres away from them watching the 'half moon of Asia over a dark granite ridge.'

The Mullah's call to prayer woke everyone at 4.30am on Easter Sunday. The day's march was straightforward apart from a crossing of the Braldu on a bridge that offered 'a frightening experience with the seething waters of the Braldu deep beneath us' (Wintersteller). The crossing recalls an incident from Diemberger's book in which he recounts an anxious conversation with the head of a local village about the state of a bridge

Hermann Buhl and some of the porters enjoying the hot springs at Chongo.

over the river. Diemberger asked if the bridge was safe and was reassured to be told that it was, as the villagers always rebuilt it just before it gave way.

Beyond the bridge the walk continued upriver over rocks worn smooth by aeons of swirling water to reach Gomboro, where the camp site lay in the lee of a stone wall. It was the high point of the fasting season and the porters celebrated the martyrdom of Muhammad's grandsons by dancing in circles, beating themselves and calling out the names of Hussein and Hassan, the Austrians finding the display wonderfully impressive. When the singing and chanting finally stopped a storm broke waking those who had managed to fall asleep.

As was becoming the norm, Wintersteller and Qader lead the expedition the following day, taking a path along the Braldu gorge with peaks of up to 6000m on each side. The journey was impressive, the path sometimes at the river's edge, at other times 100m or more above it as the Braldu flowed through a scree-filled ravine. On the way Wintersteller belied Schmuck's assessment of him as a remarkable route finder by leaving Qader at one point to forge a path through the scree, only to find that it was impossible to make progress and being forced to

The team's first view of Broad Peak.

return to a smiling companion. At 2pm the pair reached a beautiful camp site to the south of Chongo. When the porters and the rest of the team arrived the head porter, Hadschi Ismael, led the Austrians up the valley to a hot, sulphurous spring which they enjoyed jacuzzi-style. As a change from chicken and eggs the evening meal was chicken soup made from four chickens – and eggs. What Wintersteller refers to as a raven, but Schmuck dismisses as a crow, swooped down and stole an egg, Buhl yelling after it. Buhl also notes this incident in his diary so it must have made quite an impression on the Austrians, an indication, perhaps, that tensions in the team, at least on that day, were minimal. The bird clearly understood no German and escaped with its meal.

The following day the four men wasted time in the hot springs again, bathing and washing their clothes, and were forced to chase after the porters, catching them as they reached Askole at noon. Here the Satpura porters were paid off and left. They were far from happy, especially as they knew that they were to be replaced by local porters. On 25 April the Austrians weren't happy either as 7cm of snow fell and the day's trek had to be cancelled. Wintersteller was also concerned that the diet of chicken, eggs and chapattis was not only monotonous but unbalanced and possibly ruining their constitutions. Schmuck agreed, claiming he had chicken soup coming out of his ears, but the attempt to find an alternative produced only a change to baratas – chapattis fried in ghee, an unsatisfactory compromise. But another enforced rest day caused by snow and the cold was enlivened by a meal of goulash when a young deer was bought and added to the pot. Less relaxing was the first real problem with the porters. Most had no, or inadequate, footwear and the Austrians had insufficient pairs of boots for them all. Despite starting with 65 porters they now had to employ over 80 as the trekking was harder, and extra food had to be carried once civilisation had been left behind. To the expedition's 65 bags and chests of equipment they had to add a further 25 bags containing 800kg of ata (wheat flour) and 30kg of ghee as well as 100 eggs and 7kg of dried apricots. The expedition also acquired food on the hoof (four goats) and wing (nine chickens). Some of

The narrow gully leading to Camp 1. This shot was taken after the successful summit climb when Schmuck (right) and Wintersteller took Qader Saeed (left) up to the camp.

the local porters had boots which they had been given by the Herrligkoffer expedition and the choice of these rather than other men – to ease the boot problem – caused resentment, even those with boots feeling aggrieved as they were expecting to receive a second pair. Eventually everything was sorted out in the time-honoured way, those who had boots accepting 8 rupees as a fee for wearing them.

The incident with the boots is the first direct indication in Buhl's diary of problems he has with Schmuck. Buhl noted that there were too few pairs because Schmuck had left some in Salzburg and that others had been left in Skardu by Wintersteller (though it is not clear why this should have happened). Buhl complained that Schmuck had attempted to blame him for the lack, a mild enough complaint, but one which foreshadowed a much deeper complaint the following day when Buhl noted: 'Trouble among the porters, Markus (throughout his reports Buhl uses this incorrect spelling of Schmuck's first name) shouts orders, at which the porters only laugh. I tell Fritz it would be better to negotiate calmly with them, but Markus overhears this and takes me to task for criticising him. I thought that wasn't on! Markus wants to shift all responsibility to the other members. Every time there is a problem he holds Fritz responsible for it if it is food, me if it is equipment, and Kurt for anything to do with health. He just wants to play leader of the expedition and acts like Herrligkoffer.' There could hardly be a more unpleasant comment to throw at Schmuck than that comparison with Herrligkoffer, the comment certainly implying that Buhl really was embittered about the leadership.

After the boot problem was finally solved the team ate the rest of the deer and in the evening Wintersteller challenged the tallest and strongest porter to a wrestling match, winning in spectacular style with a hip throw in the first few seconds. From then on all the porters were in awe of the 'Strong Sahib'.

The weather finally improved on 26 April and the walk-in started again, following the right bank of the Braldu. Wintersteller was impressed with the ability of Qasim Ali, the lead porter, to find the best route across pathless terrain, particularly when he picked a way across the snout of the Biafo

Glacier. Schmuck seems somewhat less impressed by the porters, particularly by his inability to persuade any of them to exchange chapattis at the morning rest stop despite offering an exchange rate of one cigarette to one chapatti. At the end of the day, at Korophon, some porters could be released as the supplies they had been carrying had been used. Wintersteller was now clearly in charge of the porters as his diary notes that 'I can do without three porters', but the task of paying them off fell to Schmuck, the expedition leader. His diary notes that 'a bigmouth porter is sent back' while Wintersteller suggested that they 'try to get rid of the troublemakers.' Was the 'bigmouth' the man who declined to swap chapattis for cigarettes?

It snowed again in the night, but the trek continued the next day, Wintersteller reaching the Dumordo river first and taking off his boots and socks to wade through the glacial waters. In his diary he noted, with a hint of both pride and disgust, that the other sahibs had themselves carried across the river. The day ended at Bardumal where the tents were pitched on the fine sand of a river bed. Five more porters were sent back, the decision on which ones again resulting in tears and recriminations. Schmuck noted in his diary that Diemberger attended to the sick, his first mention of the youngest member's role as doctor. In his book Diemberger notes that his skills did not match his duties, but in a country where medical facilities were almost non-existent the presence of a doctor, even one of dubious ability, always created a ready supply of patients. Diemberger says that apart from puncturing blisters, squeezing drops in eyes and sounding chests (which must have made him look the part at least) there was little he could do. His fall-back was offering painkillers of which, thankfully, he had a ready supply. But Diemberger's skills were not sufficient to treat one porter who earlier in the day had fallen unconscious at the side of the path. Wintersteller had gone to assist the man: he had revived, but by

The route towards Camp 1. The zig-zag route of ascent contrasts sharply with the 'bum-slide' channels of the fast descent favoured by the team.

Ascending to Camp 1 on 14 May. Left to right Schmuck, Buhl and Diemberger.

Marcus Schmuck looking down the route to Camp 1 from about 5500m.

the next day was so ill that he had to be sent back, together with an escort.

For the Austrians the day's walk included the climbing of a rock tower first ascended by Erich Abram during the Italian K2 expedition trek in 1954, and an attempt to show the porters how good they were at climbing by attempting a friction slab. To his obvious disgust Schmuck was unable to reach the top. He did not say whether anyone else, notably Buhl, succeeded – but Buhl does, noting that both he and Diemberger climbed the slab, with Buhl being first to the top. As they approached Paiju the Austrians saw the Baltoro for the first time. For once Schmuck's description (a laconic observation that it is 'an edifying sight') was outclassed by that of Wintersteller who described it as being 'covered in scree and therefore black as a wall of coal 200m thick on the enormous white sandy basin of the Biafo (which feeds the Braldu).' Though impressed by the glacier it was the surroundings which held everyone's gaze: the glacier is 'flanked by the greatest granite mountains on earth, the Trango Towers, we are astounded by the singular beauty of this landscape.' That night the expedition camped at the famous wooded oasis of Paiju. Wintersteller immediately set to work organising supplies for the porters, Schmuck noting what has already become clear from the diaries of the two men, that Fritz 'is undoubtedly the hardest-working. Under a roof that protects us from the worst of the wind we sit down for dinner. Fritz then goes to the porters to cheer them up.'

At Paiju the Austrians needed to prepare the porters and loads for the trek across the Baltoro and, as leader, the job fell to Schmuck. He started to organise bundles of wood, but was soon much more interested in the discovery of a flea and then a louse on his clothes. He and Qader started a search of each other, discovering more vermin and spent time shaking louse powder into all their clothes. The horror of it all sent Schmuck to his diary to make a faithful record of events, but even then he had to break off as 'I must stop writing in order to remove a flea from my trousers. Hopefully it was the last of them – lousy times!' While the Paiju flea circus was in rehearsal, the other three climbers were off exploring the Baltoro. From both

Diemberger's book and Wintersteller's diary it is clear that they did not travel as a threesome. Wintersteller climbed 'high enough to take in the whole of the Baltoro glacier. Its dirty brown ice extends 50km eastwards to Concordia. To the left of this I see Broad Peak, with its mighty west flank, for the first time.' Diemberger and Buhl also saw the mountain, Diemberger having been thrilled that Buhl had invited him to share a reconnaissance walk. They too climbed to a high shoulder from where they could see the granite spires of the Trango Towers and, far away, Broad Peak. Interestingly Buhl does not mention seeing Broad Peak, though he does mention many of the other visible peaks. The pair arrived back at Paiju at 7.30pm, long after Wintersteller who, in the meantime, had been watching the porters again. They were making bread (chapattis): 'Pebbles the size of fists are heated in the fire, then a piece of flat dough is swiftly put around them to make balls which are put in a circle in the hot ashes. As a result the bread is baked from both the inside and the outside. They know when the bread is ready by listening for the rattle of the loose pebble. The ball is then broken, the pebble is put back in the ashes, and the bread goes into the rucsac. Today our bakers have made over 300kg of bread.'

Furthering his relationship with the porters Wintersteller joined them the following morning in a ceremony to ask for Allah's blessing on the trek along the Baltoro Glacier. Again he noticed small details about their lives – how they smoked cigarettes not by putting them in their mouths, which they never did, but 'holding them between middle and ring fingers in half-opened fists and sucking the smoke through the little opening between their crooked index fingers and their thumbs.' During the walk that day the view held the attention of the team: 'Paiju Peak and Trango Tower rise into the cloudless sky. I cannot help comparing the scene with that of the Guglia di Brenta, but this tower is four times as high and certainly much more difficult to climb' (Wintersteller). 'At every step new mountains come into view. The Trango Towers with their wild steep beauty, Liligo Peak's firn and ice shimmers, and the source of the Biafo is framed by a white sandy area that is still visible gleaming at us from the valley' (Schmuck).

It had been a sunny day, in fact oppressively hot – Wintersteller's hands had been sunburnt – and the Austrians were glad to reach the 'frequently used campsite next to heaps of scree from the endless Baltoro glacier' at Liligo where a glacial pool allowed them to wash – 'marvellous' according to Schmuck who also used the time to look for the lice that had become a special concern. Buhl noted – and Wintersteller photographed – a message scrawled on a rock near Liligo that read, in German, 'to the world's arse' with an arrow pointing towards Concordia, presumably a memento of Herrligkoffer's retreating Broad Peak team.

Though the day had been hot the night promised to be cold and the porters asked for blankets which the Austrians did not have. As Wintersteller noted, 'the lack (of blankets) will prove to have terrible consequences.' But that night the porters were pleased that Muharram had ended, singing their pleasure into the night sky, a pleasure which took the edge off the cold. Their enthusiasm lasted until the next day when, despite a light snowfall during the night, they were anxious to continue and were walking by 7.30am. But the weather was bad, fog reducing visibility and the snow increasingly deep. Wintersteller was again at the front. He slipped into a glacial stream soaking his feet, but continued to lay a trail through the knee-deep snow for the porters to follow. As they approached Urdokas Wintersteller was finally able to wring out his wet socks, after which he continued in front, now occasionally sinking through the soft snow up to his hips. The Austrians had developed a method of creating a trail for the porters which proved very effective: 'the "three footprint method". First put your foot down without using your full weight, then fix the snow lightly from the right hand side and finally put your foot down with full weight from the left hand side. This method saves energy and should make the ascent of Broad Peak much easier.' Effective the method may have been, but Wintersteller had now been out in front for much of the day and was 'already quite tired, so Qasim Ali, our experienced K2 warrior, has to step in for me from time to time.' The pair reached Urdokas at 3pm, an hour ahead of the rest of the team. It was snowing, there was a cold wind blowing and there was a limited amount of wood for warmth and cooking, so the porters were miserable when they arrived. The Austrians put up their tents but, realising that trouble was brewing, attempted to jolly the porters along by distributing sweets to them as they crouched in the shelter of the boulders.

Next day (2 May) there was indeed trouble – and it was not only confined to the porters, who refused to continue unless they were given sunglasses and tarpaulins for camping. The Austrians had only sixteen pairs of sunglasses as well as sixteen pairs of snow goggles which they wanted to keep for themselves. Schmuck decided to hand out a total of 25 pairs, fearful that to hand out everything they had would result in their being none for the climb when the porters departed. But that left around 50 porters without any form of eye protection and they refused to continue. Then those with glasses or goggles refused to walk without their companions whose eyes were unprotected: as Buhl noted: 'A model display of solidarity but very unfortunate for us.' To break the stalemate Schmuck decided on shock tactics, taking back the 25 pairs of glasses and also confiscating the boots he had handed out early in the trek. The bluff worked, the porters agreeing to continue if those without glasses were paid an extra 3 rupees. Finally at 11.30am the walk-in started again and, to the astonishment of the Austrians almost all the porters who had not been issued with goggles had now acquired them, mostly of German origin suggesting they were from Herrligkoffer's expedition.

By the time the porters started walking Wintersteller was already three and a half hours into his day's walk: realising he was adding nothing to the debate he had begun to lay trail. But there was also another reason for his departure, one that shows that the first cracks were appearing in the team. Wintersteller noted in his diary that the trail-laying 'should really be Kurt's job, but he is not willing to learn our "three footprint method" and the porters always protest violently whenever he wanted to lead.'

Around this time Schmuck also complained to Wintersteller about the behaviour of Buhl and Diemberger. The latter pair were late risers, Schmuck and Wintersteller being up early to

Camp 1. The distinctive rock tower caused Wintersteller to nickname it Tooth Camp.

Camp 1. The Tooth is further down the ridge. Left to right Schmuck, Diemberger and Buhl.

Camp 1. Wintersteller, Buhl and Diemberger look towards the camera. To the left, K2 rises above the western buttress of the Middle Peak.

organise the day's march. Often two porters would need to be held back to take down the tent Buhl and Diemberger were sharing and to help pack their gear, sometimes the tent pegs having to be pulled out as a means of rousing the pair. Schmuck had had enough and complained to Wintersteller that the two of them were being exploited. Wintersteller's response was straightforward: Buhl was still suffering from the effects of his diarrhoea and sickness, and Diemberger had 'two left hands' and so was best not helping anyway. After this interesting appraisal of his team-mates Wintersteller pointed out to Schmuck that if he (Schmuck) was going to continue calculating who had done what then it would be better if they packed up and went home. Yet despite the fine words Wintersteller was annoyed by the behaviour of the others and it was this which prompted him to avoid arguing over the trail-breaking, preferring just to get on with the job, though Buhl notes that he lost no opportunity to 'tease' Diemberger about how the recommendation that accompanied him – that he was the best ice climber in Austria – did not seem to square with his inability/unwillingness to take the lead on the trail.

It was another bad weather day. Wintersteller and Qader gave their snow goggles to two porters who were suffering, as a result of which Qader was snow-blinded. At 2pm the column stopped for a chapatti break but the bread had become wet and mushy. Buhl now took over the trail laying though at the camp site, reached at 5pm, it was Wintersteller who levelled the ground and rigged a large tarpaulin as a camp for the porters. Hearing them cough through the night he worried that things were beginning to look seriously bad. By contrast Schmuck noted that the Austrians 'warm ourselves up with tea and schnapps (and) in a happy mood we go to bed in our tent.'

On 3 May the weather improved and so the porters were willing to walk again, but only after Diemberger had administered eye drops to several who were suffering mild snow-blindness. Schmuck was now hopeful that the porters would make it all the way to their intended Base Camp, only two days' walk away. As they walked, the Austrians discussed the climbing possibilities on Masherbrum, which was now quite close: Buhl was fascinated by the peak and, according to his report, would have liked to attempt it immediately. Later, dark fog filled the valley beyond Concordia and the weather worsened. The snow deepened and although the trail was on the crest of the moraine the expedition – sahibs and porters – were often up to their knees in snow, a nightmare for the poorly-shod porters. As a result they asked Wintersteller to lay trail, his trails making life much easier for them. At the night's camp site Wintersteller, exhausted from trail laying, could not help the porters dig hollows in the snow which might have offered some shelter, so they were forced to sleep with the tarpaulin held across their bodies.

The miserable night wore the porters down and morning brought only more dreadful weather. Leaving Schmuck to deal with the remaining porters the other three Austrians started out with two of the best men, laying a trail in the hope that some or all would follow. Again Wintersteller was unhappy with

Hermann Buhl during the search for a site for Camp 2 with Fritz Wintersteller in mid-May. Wintersteller says he deliberately turned his camera to make the ground look steeper than it really was. What has not been enhanced are the clear 'perforation marks' in the snow behind and above Buhl which indicate where the snow has thought about avalanching.

Diemberger, noting that he (Wintersteller) and Buhl made trail, often through hip-deep snow, as 'Kurt is incapable of laying the track.' In his frustration Wintersteller also became annoyed with the porters and with the weather, realising that the sun, needed to bring warmth to the men and to raise their morale, was not going to appear. That night the group made camp close to Concordia.

To Base Camp

Back at the camp Schmuck had eventually persuaded the remaining porters to start out. They all reached the next camp site but it was now clear that many would make it no further. Qader was snow-blinded; Diemberger was complaining of a cold; the weather was awful; and now the porters were saying that as far as they were concerned this was Base Camp as it had taken three days from Urdokas and that Base Camp was always placed three days from there, and that they had in any case run out of food. Things looked very bleak. Next day Schmuck dismissed over 40 porters who said that they would not carry any further, giving them food for the return journey. The remaining 23 left with Buhl and Wintersteller. The two Austrians were determined to get to their proposed Base Camp, but in thick snow (and now at an altitude approaching the height of Mont Blanc) progress was painfully slow, especially as periodically the porters would stop and pray for their safety because of the conditions. When Buhl and Wintersteller waited for the porters to catch up their arrival was invariably accompanied by angry complaints and so the Austrians eventually decided to push ahead regardless. At 3pm, realising that further progress was pointless, they set up a camp in a protected hollow, the porters arriving some time later, angry and exhausted. Wintersteller calmed them down with hot tea while Buhl attempted to make radio contact with Schmuck back at Concordia. The attempt was a failure. At the Concordia camp, having watched porters leave in both directions, Schmuck enjoyed a half-day's peace, and then, with Diemberger, a relaxing meal.

The peace was not to last. On 6 May Buhl and Wintersteller failed to persuade the porters at their camp to continue despite the tea they made for them. They attempted to reach Schmuck on the radio, but again failed and watched as the porters headed down, not knowing if they would see them or any others again. Then, determined to do something positive, the pair put on snowshoes and headed towards their intended Base Camp. The weather improved, K2 catching the sun gloriously, and at a large boulder dragged to the spot by the glacier they decided they had found the ideal Base Camp site and headed back to their last camp where they dried their sodden clothes in the sun.

At the lower camp Schmuck's radio was receiving intermittently, but obviously not transmitting. He heard that the porters had left camp, but did not know whether they were heading up or down. That question was emphatically answered at 10am when the porters arrived at camp, angrily demanding their money and saying that they were all leaving. Schmuck tried to reason with them, but apart from two (who were retained to act as mailrunners, but would also work as porters) they were all adamant. They demanded food for the journey, but Schmuck told them that they should have been more frugal with what they had. He also confiscated the sunglasses that had been given to them: no bluff this time, just a reminder of who was in charge. Apart from the mailrunners the porters then left, still angry and shouting threats over their shoulders. Schmuck, wearied by the long battles was now in despair. His expedition had 1200kgs of equipment stacked 20kms away from Base Camp and only the four team members, Qader and two mailrunners/porters (Machmad Ali and Hakim Koli: the two were brothers) left to shift it. Perhaps seeing the need for action, Diemberger decided to make a start with the load shifting and headed off with the first load. The two porters followed with Qader, Schmuck bringing up the rear. That night the expedition huddled into two tents at the top camp: only the porters - now in a tent rather than under tarpaulin - seemed to have been pleased with the situation.

Time was now critical. There were 40 loads at the lower camp, 25 at the top one and the seven men had to move them as fast as

Wintersteller and Buhl on their way from Camp 1 to Camp 2 during the first attempt on the summit.

Camp 2 beneath the cornice.

possible or their chance on the mountain would vanish. Over the next week or so the men made daily trips between the camps. On 8 May Buhl and Wintersteller carried loads (now weighing up to 35kg in order to reduce the number of carries) to Base Camp, then returned to take another two up. Wintersteller's weary diary entry for the day was 'Sahib as porter.' On 9 May the two men spent their first night at Base Camp after another exhausting day of load carrying. The day was beautiful, starting very cold (-7°C) but clear, and in the evening 'the mountains are illuminated by the wonderful reddish glow of the evening sun. Broad Peak and K2 stand out sharply against the already dark sky, seeming strangely close' (Wintersteller). That night the summit of Broad Peak was still 3200m above them.

Next day Wintersteller and Buhl did not get up until 8am. The previous day they had walked 24km in bad conditions, carrying loads of 30kg for half the distance. They were now operating at almost 5000m and the effort had drained them, though what they had achieved suggests that Buhl had now recovered from his sickness. He organised the camp while Wintersteller did what he did best – he cooked. The other five soon arrived with more loads, leaving again immediately. Later Buhl and Wintersteller also dropped down to collect loads, all seven men returning to Base Camp and spending the night there. Yet despite Buhl and Wintersteller having operated as a team for several days, that night the old order was re-established, with Buhl and Diemberger in one tent, Schmuck and Wintersteller in another.

By now Wintersteller was in remarkable condition, what Schmuck called in his diary 'super porter mode.' He was covering the distance downhill between the camps in an astonishing 50 minutes (good jogging speed) without his pulse rate going above 80 beats per minute, and hauling back loads of over 35kg. He had fixed the radios (battery problems) and was routinely cooking breakfast – usually porridge and Ovaltine – and lunch – hash browns for the climbers, peas, bacon and onions for the porters - and often dinner as well. He was concerned about the diet that was being forced on the three Muslims as it included not only bacon, but salami and tinned pork as well, but wryly noted in his diary that high on the mountain Allah is required to turn not one, but two blind eyes. (When Qader Saeed heard this suggestion in Salzburg many years later he was quick to point out that in his opinion none of the porters were ever given pork or bacon.)

Gradually the Concordia camp was carried to the depot camp and the loads were then moved through to Base Camp so that by 12 May, an enforced rest day as the weather turned sour again (a snowstorm stopping the two mailrunners from crossing the Baltoro), the team was in a position to think about climbing the mountain. On that day Wintersteller finally relaxed, playing chess with Schmuck while Buhl cooked meat and rice for lunch (and, poignantly, wrote a Mother's Day card to his wife).

Looking out from Camp 2.

The diaries of Schmuck give an idea of the state of the Austrians by the time the real climb began. Schmuck was worn out by the effort of organisation and by the continual arguing with the porters. The expedition to that point had not studied his capabilities as a climber, only those as man manager and these had put a strain on a man who, until then, had only experienced outings with small groups of friends. His diary, so lyrical in the early days, had now become a mere listing of the day's events and problems. By contrast Wintersteller, who had never before travelled far from home (apart from the Spitsbergen expedition), had blossomed like the apricot trees the team had passed. He had also showed that his strength, the main reason he had been chosen, had not diminished as he had climbed higher. Buhl had begun slowly: illness had weakened him during the early stages, but towards the end of the walk-in the stamina and iron will that are the basis of his legend had appeared. He had also noted in his diary – 'Am in good shape'. Diemberger's status is more difficult to define. His refusal or inability to help with trail making for the porters had not translated into an unwillingness to work hard when the loads needed shifting to Base Camp. His relationship with Buhl is also enigmatic. Diemberger's version is that he and Buhl had become friends, the friendship developing after Buhl had taken him under his wing, and that he was keen to learn from the more experienced man. The tale Schmuck and Wintersteller tell does not support this, suggesting rather that the young Diemberger, an ambitious climber, was grasping the chance of spending time with a man of whom he was in awe in the hope that something might rub off. It would be no disrespect to suggest this: virtually the whole climbing world was in awe of Buhl, including Marcus Schmuck even though he was one of the closest to him in terms of raw climbing ability. Qader Saeed agrees with the Schmuck–Wintersteller view, believing that because the young, inexperienced Diemberger was the outsider of the group – the others knowing each other to a lesser or greater degree – he had latched on to Buhl who tolerated him, but did not actually like him much.

Qader, Schmuck and Wintersteller also suggest that Buhl became increasingly irritated with Diemberger's attention and

had begun to criticise the young climber's abilities and performance, occasionally reducing Diemberger to tears with his critical
and belittling jibes. Diemberger does not disagree that Buhl
could be, and was, cruel. He was as hard on others as he was on
himself, says Diemberger, and it is true that Buhl occasionally
upset him. However, although Buhl's diary does note once
'small argument with Kurt', it does not elaborate on the cause
and is an isolated entry for the walk-in phase of the expedition.
It is also the case that Buhl and Diemberger were usually sharing a tent. This may contradict the Schmuck–Wintersteller view,
or may merely be a reflection of the strain on Schmuck. Though
Buhl was Schmuck's friend, that friendship was built as much
on mutual respect as climbers and the need, each for the other,
of a partner of comparable talent. Now with Schmuck exhausted by expedition leadership and perhaps also by an undercur-
rent of antagonism he felt emanated from Buhl, a consequence
of the leadership issue, he seems to have sought comfort in a
more established friendship, one with someone whose attitude
to the expedition was much simpler. Wintersteller was simply
overjoyed to be there, happy with the privilege of being there.
Faced with the inevitable competitiveness of Buhl and the aspi-
rations of Diemberger, Schmuck was grateful for the compan-
ionship of a man who was just glad to be with him.

To Broad Peak

On 13 May the Austrian Karakoram expedition finally set off on
the journey they had planned. Without porters they headed
towards the western face of Broad Peak. It was the closest face
to them, but they had already realised that Dyhrenfurth's view
that the spur which split the western face and reached the snowfield below the col between the main and central summits
offered a feasible route to the top. Schmuck says that Buhl
favoured a route up the snow flank to the north of the ridge, but
this proved to be constantly threatened by ice falls from 2000m
above and so a more southerly route was chosen.

On the first approach Wintersteller, cook and kitchen organiser, started after the other three, catching them at the foot of the

K2 from Camp 2. The camp had a toilet which faced the world's second highest peak, though this shot was, sadly, not taken from there.

A wonderfully atmospheric shot by Fritz Wintersteller. It was taken from Camp 2 on the second, successful attempt on the summit. To the left is Broad Col, with cliffs leading to the headwall of the Forepeak directly above.

spur. The four now took turns breaking trail, finally reaching the base of a 150m-high gully barely 2m wide and at an angle of 50°. They climbed this, sinking in snow up to their hips and eventually reached a promontory at a height which Wintersteller and Buhl guessed as 5500m, but Schmuck thought only 5300m. It was 11.45am. The three early starters had been climbing at a rate of between 100m–170m/hour depending on which height is assumed. Given that they had also had to walk to the base of the spur this shows that they were in good shape. At the promontory Marcus Schmuck, exhausted by the climb and having forgotten his gloves – the weather that first day being excellent – decided to turn back. At this point Buhl notes that his feet were 'ice-cold, without feeling'. But leaving some of his load behind, he continued with Diemberger and Wintersteller climbing through knee-deep snow at an angle of 45° to reach a saddle at about 5800m where a small platform of rubble would make an excellent camp site. This would be Camp 1, which Wintersteller christened Tooth Camp after a prominent spire of rock. The three then slipped and slid their way down, reaching the Baltoro Glacier in just 30 minutes.

All four men were tired from their exertions, the sun waking them next day much later than they usually rose. Wintersteller cooked a breakfast of ham and eggs and then did the washing up as the others headed off towards the peak again. Using the prepared trail Wintersteller caught the trio up below the promontory and took over the trail breaking. He laid, he said, a flatter trail to make it easier for the others, Schmuck appreciating the effort as he noted that 'Fritz lays a gently rising, easily managed track' to the Tooth Camp. There Schmuck and Wintersteller bashed out a platform for the tents while Buhl and Diemberger continued up to explore the route. When the platform was ready, the effort making both men breathe heavily, the two headed down, reaching the Baltoro in just 20 minutes (for a descent of 800m) by sliding on their backsides. Wintersteller again turned cook, preparing a meal of meat and cabbage which was ready when Buhl and Diemberger arrived. The latter pair had climbed 200m above Camp 1, reaching 6100m, but reported that the spur was covered in pure ice above 6000m and that it would be better to find a way to the right, traversing a glacial hollow to reach a plateau below the snowfield leading to the Wind Gap (Broad Col) between the main and middle peaks.

Wintersteller was up first again the next day making a breakfast of bacon, eggs and cocoa while Schmuck washed his feet in snow. As usual Wintersteller did the washing up too, taking time to clean the soot off a big cooking pot before setting out after the others. As before he caught them near the promontory and renewed the track to Camp 1. Today Buhl and Diemberger

Hermann Buhl at the fixed ropes left by the Herrligkoffer expedition.

were having bad days (Buhl's diary notes that he found the climb 'very exhausting') and Schmuck was also very tired. As a consequence Diemberger and Schmuck went down immediately, again taking only 20 minutes to reach the Baltoro. Buhl and Wintersteller, who planned to stay at Camp 1 the next day, did further work at the camp before descending. At Base Camp they prepared their personal equipment for the following day. That night Buhl noted – 'Ate well, slept badly, brooded too much', an enigmatic entry. What was he brooding about?

On 16 May Wintersteller's early morning culinary delight was custard after which the four started towards Camp 1. Buhl and Wintersteller were now carrying very heavy loads (personal gear as well as equipment for further up the mountain) and Wintersteller was angered when Diemberger, who was having a particularly bad day, said that 'next time I'm not moving unless all the rucsacs are checked and the weight equally distributed.' Wintersteller noted in his diary that 'We had never discussed how much each of us should carry. Anyway, a change of rucsac would have been fatal for him because there is no way that he had the heaviest one. It was noticeable that with him, when something went wrong it was always someone else's fault. He never considered that he himself might be to blame.' The aggravation that had begun on the walk-in was beginning to show itself again. It is noticeable too that it was Fritz Wintersteller who showed his frustration. He had been cook and labourer without pause or complaint for days, and felt personally aggrieved that someone was suggesting that others were not pulling their weight. His diary was written during the evening: at the time he must have pushed his annoyance to one side, acting as cook yet again after Schmuck and Diemberger descended, leaving him with Buhl at Camp 1. There, whatever had been troubling Buhl the night before seems to have dissipated, his diary entry noting 'Great mood.' The entry might have indicated relief. In conversation with Wintersteller it is clear that he had much less respect for Buhl than either Schmuck or Diemberger. Wintersteller shared the view of others that Buhl had been wrong to break his Nanga Parbat contract and later made a point of showing Buhl that he (Wintersteller) was the stronger man. Perhaps Buhl was already concerned about their relationship and was pleasantly surprised at how well it had turned out.

Down at Base Camp Qader Saeed had taken over the job of cooking the evening meal, serving Diemberger and Schmuck with bread, potatoes and tea. The radios, once the source of frustration, were working well allowing the four men to keep in contact as night fell and a huge avalanche crashed down the side of K2.

Having made radio contact with Base Camp at 8am Buhl and Wintersteller left Camp 1 at 9am, not lightly loaded just to explore the route, but fully loaded as they intended, if possible, to establish Camp 2. Wintersteller's diary entry for the day told the story of a far from straightforward climb: 'At 10.30 we traverse into the glacial hollow and have great difficulty climbing any further in the knee-deep snow. Now the slope rears up, becoming ever steeper. For each step forward one must put one's foot down three times in order to have a starting position for the next step. I try again and again to traverse left in order to reach the plateau. Again and again I am forced to the right, until finally, just under a cornice, we manage to cross a 50° slope on a very exposed route. On the plateau (at 6450m) a stiff wind forces us back under the cornice. We decide to erect Camp 2 under the 5m wide ice roof of the cornice and begin to prepare the site so that we can quickly put up a tent. We then slide down to Tooth Camp in 45 minutes.' Buhl and Wintersteller had pushed the route out a further 650m and established Camp 2, a great day's effort. Although his diary entry for the day does not say as much, Buhl did not share Wintersteller's enthusiasm for the site of Camp 2, a later entry complaining about the site and suggesting that it was used against his better judgement. He did, however, share Wintersteller's satisfaction in a good day's work noting that in the evening there was 'a great atmosphere' in the tent.

That day Schmuck (who was concerned about one of his knees which 'doesn't seem to be up to this kind of strain') and Diemberger had carried loads up to Camp 1 from where they had been able to talk to the lead climbers. Encouraged by their

progress the two slid back to Base Camp where Qader had prepared 'wonderful food.'

On 18 May Buhl and Wintersteller climbed back up to Camp 2
(Cornice Camp as Wintersteller calls it in his diary) again carrying big loads. They enlarged the site and inspected the cornice
to satisfy themselves that it was safe. The site had the advantage
of being in the sun in the afternoon (from noon to 7.30pm), the
tents becoming very warm which made for pleasant evening
meal times. But it did not receive any morning sun and so was
cold when the climbers rose and also had the disadvantage of
being in what was effectively a wind tunnel. As a result in bad
weather snow was driven hard across it. Having levelled the site
the pair slid back down to Camp 1 satisfied that the next day
they would have the camp ready for occupation.

At Base Camp Diemberger prepared breakfast and after radio
contact with the lead climbers he and Schmuck set off for Camp
1 for the sixth time. For Schmuck the climb was getting easier, if
more monotonous: 'I breathe through my nose, with each step
one breath, breathing in as I lift my foot, breathing out as I set it
down. My speed is regulated by the steepness, but all the way
to Camp 1 I can maintain this way of breathing.' The pair slid
down as usual, but found Base Camp deserted as Qader had
gone down to find more fuel at the equipment dump below.
Unable to brew tea, the two men drank beer and ate cheese with
paprika and pepper – 'it tastes delicious.' In the evening they sat
in Schmuck's tent (they were not sharing a tent) and looked
through Dyhrenfurth's Baltoro book by candlelight. Each was
entranced by the picture of Hidden Peak (Gasherbrum I). They
could enjoy their lazy evening as the next day they were moving up to Camp 1 and did not intend to start until the afternoon.

Schmuck tidied Base Camp the following day, noting in his
diary before he left the camp that he 'wants to come back having reached the top. This is perhaps an immodest thought, but
maybe the weather god will smile on us.' Before leaving he tried
to make radio contact with Camp 1 but failed and assumed that
Buhl and Wintersteller were also having a lazy morning (he was
wrong). Then, for the seventh time Schmuck and Diemberger
climbed to Camp 1, arriving in a snow flurry at 6pm.

Abseiling down the fixed ropes towards Camp 2.

Camp 1 was empty. Buhl and Wintersteller had left at 7.30am, anxious to make the most of a poor day. Despite very heavy loads they had arrived at Camp 2 at 11.30am, their tracks of the previous day being intact. At the camp the two men had to clear snow and also to make the platform bigger so that a second tent could be accommodated. Wintersteller estimated that by the time they had finished they had (over the three days) shifted 16 cubic metres of snow, a testament to their excellent acclimatisation and fitness. As well as the tents they had also constructed a toilet – one with a view of K2. What more could a man ask!

Their work completed they headed up for a quick reconnaissance of the plateau. It did not look good. Most of the slope was pure ice rather than snow – so there would be nothing to slide down, which meant longer times to retreat – and a scan of the route suggested they might have problems finding a site for

Camp 3. Wintersteller was not happy, but his frame of mind improved during the evening: 'It's already dark on the Godwin-Austin glacier while here we linger in the warm light of the evening sun and admire the peaks: K2, Angel, Crystal and Marble Peak, Masherbrum and, in the distance, Paiju Peak. We then enjoy our first night in Cornice Camp.'

Next day Buhl and Wintersteller rose early. The night before they had made a vacuum flask of drink and Wintersteller drank it dry swearing that never again would he drink coffee late in the evening, four visits to the K2 toilet having been needed in the night, exhausting and dehydrating him. Setting off downhill Wintersteller arrived at Camp 1 in time to act as an alarm clock for Schmuck and Diemberger. He made them a breakfast of sausage and bread while Schmuck made tea for everyone. By 9am all four men were on their way back up to Camp 2, reaching it after three hours of hard effort with Buhl and Wintersteller, clearly better acclimatised, making trail. Wintersteller cooked lunch, then Schmuck and Diemberger descended. The weather had by now turned nasty and Schmuck was chastened by the descent: 'I don't feel very confident on the 150m, almost 50° snow-covered slope that leads up to the cornice. We carefully trudge down and arrive safely in the hollow. The storm doesn't ease off – frozen faces – careful now, the danger of avalanches is high. The weather then improves and we carefully lay a track across the windslabs, sheer ice and crevasses to Camp 1.' From above, Wintersteller's view of that first slope was quite different. He believed it was only 35° and was appalled to see Diemberger facing in to downclimb on a section that 'Hermann and I had comfortably walked down that morning.' His disparagement is clear: 'Kurt, Austria's greatest ice climber, master of the Königsspitze mushroom, hesitates.'

After enjoying Diemberger's discomfort Wintersteller joined Buhl in another exploration of the plateau above the camp. They went higher and were delighted to discover an equipment dump from Herrligkoffer's 1954 expedition. There were ropes, climbing gear, a tent and food. Wintersteller does not say what the food comprised, but in his book Diemberger says it included salami, bacon and a bottle of egg-liqueur which the Austro-

German team had discovered at the Italian 1954 K2 expedition base camp. From Italy to the base of K2, then across the Baltoro and half-way up Broad Peak, a sojourn in the snow at over 6000m and now into the stomachs of the Austrians. The food was, says Diemberger, perfectly preserved in the world's highest freezer.

Buhl and Wintersteller were finally driven back by snow: a storm had arrived, one which increased in strength during the night. At Camp 1, by dawn, Schmuck and Diemberger were ragged from lack of sleep but prepared themselves to carry further loads up to Camp 2. They waited for Buhl and Wintersteller to arrive, but when they did not the two started up, bashing a trail through deep snow. At the base of the final slope they saw Buhl and Wintersteller working at the camp site. Schmuck was angered when they did not come down to help with the trail breaking and harsh words were said at the camp. Wintersteller (after a solid night's sleep which he put down to a decision to drink tea rather than coffee) and Buhl had made a trail up to the Herrligkoffer dump and brought down more equipment. Then, at Camp 2 Wintersteller had cleared the fresh snow from the site. But the idea had been to carry loads up from Camp 1 and so despite these efforts there was a sharp exchange of views between the two pairs. At the end peace was restored and, in view of the weather, the four decided to descend to Base Camp for a rest, after first going back up to the Herrligkoffer dump. Schmuck and Wintersteller left immediately after they returned from the dump, reaching Base Camp in the early evening after a descent of over 1600m. Buhl and Diemberger arrived later: after Schmuck and Wintersteller departed they had climbed to around 6700m to look at the route. It had been a dangerous solo effort, Buhl's diary noting: 'The ropes from H. [fixed ropes from the Herrligkoffer expedition] are partly frozen into the ice, up to 15cm deep and have to be freed laboriously centimetre by centimetre. Without a safety rope and without steps in the sheer, rock-hard ice which slopes at an angle of about 55°, it is not easy, with only the rope cut from the ice to hold on to as we work with our ice axes. The ropes are still in good condition. By 12.30 we are at about 6700m, 250m above the plateau. A heavy snowstorm then starts so I turn back, sliding down the rope which I secured with an axe.'

At Base Camp everyone rested for a day writing their diaries, or postcards to expedition sponsors. As usual Wintersteller acted as cook and also mended the team's two typewriters. In the evening he noted that there was anger over Diemberger's neglect of his duties as doctor: 'I don't get the Ichthyol I need for an abscess between my toes and the others don't get their vitamin pills regularly. Instead of accepting our criticism and getting on with his job as orderly, he uses the same stupid excuses again and again, and that drives us all up the wall.' Buhl notes the same argument in his diary, so it must have been serious. He ends his entry with a single word: *Moralpredigt*! The kindest translation would be to suggest that a 'moral sermon' had been administered. Buhl does not elaborate on who gave and who received the admonition, but the exclamation mark seems to imply that it was Diemberger to him, the '!' being added in the nature of 'what a cheek!'

Wintersteller continued to give voice to his displeasure with Diemberger, adding that 'Qader is also annoyed with him because he (Diemberger) is always going to him with special demands.' Of the four Austrians Diemberger was the only one who spoke reasonable English. Schmuck's English (then as now) was poor, Wintersteller's better, but not much better. Buhl, says Qader, spoke almost no English at all. Diemberger therefore tended to be the bridge between Qader and the Austrians and vice versa. In conversation with Qader it seems that this was not a problem at first, but eventually Qader tired of Diemberger's habit of seeking special, personal favours as though they were team requests. Exaggerating things to his own advantage, as Qader put it.

Next day, perhaps to get away from possible trouble, Wintersteller went down to the equipment dump and the camp beyond that to bring back fuel, a cooker and spare parts, and some cigarettes for himself. He also collected skis and enjoyed himself skiing back to Base Camp, not arriving until 6.30pm. Even so he was back before Buhl and Diemberger. Their quarrel patched up, the pair had spent a long day looking for

Herrligkoffer's base camp in the hope of being able to salvage more equipment and food. With all the fresh snow a real search was almost impossible and they found no trace. Buhl was impressed by the view of Broad Peak from the 1954 base area, but not by the route: 'The valley is terribly romantic, but far too dangerous for ascent because of the hanging glaciers.'

Undaunted by their lack of success, the following day Buhl and Diemberger headed off towards K2 in the hope of finding the Italian 1954 base camp and, perhaps, more goodies. That search also failed as it snowed almost all day. From that side Buhl noted that Broad Peak was 'very hostile'. Schmuck was still resting as he had injured a foot on the mountain. He acted as cook for the day (cooking deer goulash: the previous day the team had eaten goat goulash) while Wintersteller mended his camera. When Buhl and Diemberger returned Wintersteller was again aggravated by the younger man's attitude: 'Kurt seems very sullen. He is worried about the equipment in the depot at the foot of the peak. Tomorrow he wants to fetch the crampons in case they are buried by avalanches. Hopefully that'll make him feel better.'

On 25 May Diemberger did indeed go to the foot of the climb to rescue the crampons. The weather had improved but on all sides avalanches were thundering into the valley. The Austrians were keen to be off to Broad Peak again as soon as possible, but were forced to wait patiently for the snow to stabilise. So they wasted time taking advertising photographs, especially those for companies which had sponsored them with food – 'something we should have done long ago' (Wintersteller). They all hoped that the mailrunners would arrive, though that seemed a doubtful possibility, the deep new snow probably preventing them from getting through. Just to be active Schmuck went skiing, slaloming down the side of the moraine and frequently calling out that he could see the mailrunners, much to the annoyance of the others. One last time he shouted the same thing – the others ignored him, but this time the runners really did appear. They were utterly exhausted and Hakim Koli was suffering from the effects of a fall into a river from which he had had to be rescued, almost dead, by his brother. But the joy of the runners' arrival was short-lived. For all but Buhl and Qader it would have been better had the runners not arrived. Buhl had letters – two, one of them, according to Schmuck, not very nice though he gives no details (and neither does Buhl). Qader had eight letters and two pairs of boots. For the others the disappointment was far worse than the agonies of anticipation. This was particularly true for Schmuck as he was hoping for news from his family. That evening the weather was superb. With the barometer indicating a change for the better the Austrians prepared to go back on the hill the following day.

Camp 3 (the Eagle's Nest). To the left is Chogolisa while beyond the tent is Mitre Peak.

4
The Forepeak

On 26 May the Austrians left Base Camp: everything was ready. If the weather held they were off to climb Broad Peak. They started out at 5am and for once Wintersteller was having a bad day, the other three sharing the trail breaking – with Diemberger doing rather more than his share according to Buhl – as far as Camp 1 which they reached at 9am (about 900m in four hours, but with some horizontal distance as well). At the camp they ate and packed more supplies. In his diary Schmuck noted that their rucsacs weighed between 12kg and 22kg without saying who was carrying which. After the meal Wintersteller recovered and led towards Camp 2.

In his diary Buhl noted Wintersteller's trail breaking, but only after pointing out that he (Buhl) had been leading at first, with Wintersteller following him, not in his trail, but making his own. Buhl noted: 'Typical Fritz. I take appropriate action, continuing behind him.' Buhl expanded on the incident in one of his reports: 'Fritz must be in top shape I think to myself, and if he has so much surplus energy why shouldn't he be the one making the trail – so I fall in behind. It's fine by me and Fritz can work off some of his ambition.' This may not have been the first time this had happened, and it happened again later, as we shall see.

The sun was now merciless, sapping the men's energy and will, and slowing them to a crawl. At the base of the final slope to Camp 2 they were stopped by an obvious windslab avalanche danger. To minimise the danger Buhl, who took over the lead,

Fritz Wintersteller's original photograph is labelled 'Adlerhorst Idylle', the Eagle's Nest idyll.

shed his rucsac and climbed straight up to the cornice, before breaking left to reach the camp. Wintersteller followed, but had severe problems. He was much heavier than Buhl, even without the load he was carrying, and constantly sank into the soft snow. The physical and mental effort exhausted him and he arrived at the camp utterly spent. Schmuck and Diemberger followed, Diemberger then descending to bring up his rucsac as he had first climbed up with Buhl's. The camp had to be excavated from 1m of fresh snow, but Wintersteller could only watch as the other three started digging. To compensate he cooked a meal. One of the tents had been ripped by the weight of fallen snow: it was lucky that they had acquired a spare from the Herrligkoffer dump. In his report Buhl again complained about the siting of the camp: 'My reservations were all too well founded, but this is no time to quarrel. Instead we must free the tents from the snow, which must weigh a ton.'

Next day, at 6am Schmuck and Wintersteller slid down to Camp 1 to collect more equipment, Schmuck being unable to keep up with the revitalised Wintersteller. By 7.30am the two had packed their loads and were on their way back up, reaching Camp 2 again at 10.15am. Meanwhile Buhl and Diemberger had worked on the Camp 2 site, and then started to prepare the route above, climbing to the Herrligkoffer dump and continuing. At Camp 2 Wintersteller cooked pasta with cheese, meat and tomato puree, but the two lead climbers were so engrossed in their work (on what Diemberger in his book describes as polished ice) that they did without a midday meal, recalling Schmuck's opinion of climbing with Buhl – that it was necessary to eat before setting out. In the afternoon Schmuck slept in the warmth of the sun, while Wintersteller climbed up alone to take photographs. Buhl's view of this can be judged from his diary entry: 'Markus and Fritz back in Camp II again. Inexplicably they stay there the whole day although I had ordered them to come after us with loads, carrying them as high as possible. Once one of them ascends to the plateau, but then goes back to the camp.'

Wintersteller says that Buhl and Diemberger called down that they were short of rope, so he went back to Camp 2 from where he and Schmuck carried ropes and tents up to the Herrligkoffer dump. On their way up they passed the descending Buhl – 'They come towards me with loads. Short, impolite greetings and sharp words are uttered on both sides and they climb on' (Buhl). It seems that Buhl's decision to assert his authority as climbing leader had not gone down too well. From the dump back down to Camp 2 a rope was fixed to aid the steep descent. That night all four men slept at Camp 2, Buhl noting that 'we swallowed our resentment with our evening meal.'

On 28 May the four men carried their personal gear, weighing around 16kg, as far as the Herrligkoffer dump. As Buhl and Diemberger were making the trail, Schmuck and Wintersteller also carried cooking equipment, airbeds and other camping equipment. They dropped off these supplies and went back for more, leaving the route forging to Buhl and Diemberger, Buhl noting that he started alone because 'Kurt is not ready, as usual'. He mentions Diemberger again in the same passage: 'Kurt hacks steps – I am not very convinced of his skills as an ice climber.' On the second load carry Wintersteller passed the leaders who were descending to fetch more loads. He then climbed beyond their high point hoping to find a place for Camp 3. At 7100m he found a place among rocks (and immediately christened it, just as he had with Camps 1 and 2, calling it the Eagle's Nest). As the team were hoping for something higher Wintersteller pushed on, but soon realised that on the 30° slope there was unlikely to be a better site. He therefore returned to the first site and set down his load. The others soon appeared with the rest of the equipment for the camp. Schmuck had had an epic day. Descending for the second time towards Camp 2 he had been hit by rocks and knocked unconscious. Luckily he was clipped into the fixed rope and came to hanging from it, his left hand swinging uselessly by his side. For a fearful moment it looked as though his own expedition was over, but gradually life returned to the hand and after a long rest he was able to resume climbing. Perhaps as a result of this loss of time Wintersteller's personal gear had been left behind at the Herrligkoffer dump, as had the cooking stuff (which everyone seems by now to have assumed was Wintersteller's personal responsibility) and he had to go

Schmuck (foreground) and Buhl at Camp 3 on 8 June 1957.

down the 300m to the dump on his own to collect it. He did not return until 7.30pm when he was treated to comments about the lack of food as a result of the delay.

In his report Buhl devoted many lines to this incident: 'We are hungry and so we quickly organise a cooking site. But to our dismay we don't have any cooking pots. "Damn it, Fritz has them in his rucsac!" Well, where is he then? "Just gone down to get his second load." We might have to wait a long time – and we do, waiting in the cold for more than an hour. The sun was already setting and all we could do was enjoy the view, shiver and, now and again, curse Fritz. "He could have gone down earlier, he had the whole day to do it." It was taking too long for me, especially as it was already getting dark and so I descended and met him by the final fixed rope. Naturally he wasn't bothered and so there's no point arguing.' Given that Wintersteller had already made trail to the camp site and then gone back for another load this seems very unfair.

After the evening meal Diemberger made tea and Ovaltine non-stop for two and a half hours and was highly praised by the others which further enraged the normally placid Wintersteller.

In fact this incident seems to have been a piece of amateur psychology on the part of Schmuck (and, possibly, Buhl). In his diary Schmuck notes Diemberger's efforts, but adds that it is 'the first thing he does for the team.' Despite their diaries making it clear that Diemberger was involved in the load-carrying to establish the lower camps, it is equally clear from conversations with Schmuck and Wintersteller (and from Wintersteller's diary) that Diemberger's reluctance to play a full role in the effort – his refusal to break trail for the porters and increased truculence on the mountain – had begun to alienate them and was having a detrimental effect on team spirit. It seems that Schmuck had decided to try verbal rewards in the hope this might bring about a change.

The four did not attempt to sleep until 10.30pm. It was so cold that they all slept with their boots on to avoid them freezing. They slept well, but Buhl was awake by 2am, rousing the others and suggesting that they should be on their way. It is no surprise that Buhl wanted an early start. His experience on Nanga Parbat would have reminded him that the rate of ascent declined as altitude increased. The Austrians had wanted to set Camp 3 higher, but had not been able to and so there was still a climb of over 900m to the summit. Buhl would have known that they would do well to reach the summit and return in daylight unless they started very early. He was also, according to Schmuck and Wintersteller, ill, the diarrhoea and sickness which had affected him early in the trip, and intermittently throughout it, having returned. However, this assessment of Buhl's condition is disputed by Diemberger who claims that Buhl's problems on the day – and on the later summit climb – were caused by the cold affecting the foot which had been frostbitten on Nanga Parbat.

Neither Buhl's diary nor his reports make any mention of his having had diarrhoea on the climb. Buhl does say that he had it early in the trip, but there is no further mention. However, his report does indicate that all was not well with him, and that as the hours passed until they actually got underway things did not improve: 'I must confess I don't feel the excitement, the enthusiasm, the anticipatory rush that I felt on the days preceding my ascent of Nanga Parbat. I slept well, but at 1am I woke and could not get back to sleep. I could feel the cold coming through the wall of the tent and at 2am it took a great effort to tear myself from my sleeping bag and rouse the others. But for them it is just too early. Nobody stirs, the cold keeping them in their bags as if hypnotised. It is another hour before Fritz begins cooking, and that goes very slowly. Every half-hour a mug of hot tea is delivered to our tent. Too little fluid for a long day. The cold has a paralysing effect on everyone. I lie fully clothed in the tent and wait till it gets light. Yesterday Fritz was supposed to have brought up a rope, but unfortunately didn't so we don't have one. Fritz thinks that without one the final ridge might be too risky. Despite the darkness, I try to descend to retrieve the last fixed rope, but it's too dangerous – I can't see more than 10m ahead. Markus asks when we are going to leave, but we all find the cold absolutely paralysing. It is easily -25°C, perhaps -30, and on top of that there is a cold wind. Finally when it is light I go to fetch the rope. When I get back Fritz and Markus have already gone. Kurt is still there, tidying things up.' Buhl's diary entry adds further details, some of them enigmatic: 'I want to descend to get the last fixed rope because Fritz is not in a rational frame of mind, but it is still too dark. So I wait until dawn. Outside it is freezing. I seem to lack the motivation to do anything and everyone else pretty much does what he wants. That's what the last two days have done. Then Markus asks, what about starting? Fine with me – I woke them up at 2am, didn't I? So I descend to fetch the rope and when I return Fritz and Markus have gone, though Kurt is still there. It is 6am, a wonderful day, though a bit windy and bitingly cold, maybe -25°C to -30°C. In my opinion our departure is too late, but Markus said that it wouldn't be possible to go earlier because of the cold. The climbing is good, ice at first, then hard snow with little hidden crevasses. I take two breaths for each step.'

Having attempted to exercise his climbing leadership yesterday Buhl was now willing to let others make decisions. Fritz was 'not rational', presumably because he wanted to take a rope, which seems sensible enough. Buhl wanted to start early, but Marcus said no and so the start was delayed. For whatever reason, Buhl was having a bad day.

Schmuck says that the early part of the climb, up a steep, ice-shrouded slope, was accomplished in light reflected from K2. Can any climbers have ever had so glorious a source to illuminate their efforts? When they reached a less steep snowfield the wind picked up, chilling them further. At 7400m they were forced to stop, rubbing their legs and stamping their feet to get some warmth back into them, and then putting on windproof trousers and overboots, the latter to combat the frightening cold of the powder snow through which they now had to break trail. The powder stopped them from taking a direct line upwards, forcing them to the left, with Schmuck and Wintersteller still making the track and Buhl and Diemberger following them. At this stage the two leaders were not concerned with the fact that they were trail making, being anxious to keep moving as movement equalled warmth. They climbed up towards the sun and when they met it they stopped, removed their boots and rubbed life back into their feet. When Buhl and Diemberger arrived Schmuck asked that they should go into the lead to relieve himself and Wintersteller. In his diary Schmuck noted his amazement and aggravation when Diemberger refused to take over. Schmuck pointed out that Wintersteller was always ready to lead. Perhaps to ease the tension created by the exchange Buhl went into the lead, making trail up to a crevasse which blocked the way to the final slope below the Wind Gap.

Although the diaries of Buhl, Schmuck and Wintersteller are not explicit at this point it is clear from what follows that they called up Diemberger and pointed out that as he has been offered to them as a brilliant ice climber it was now time to prove it. Diemberger 'walks to and fro along the edge of the crevasse and tells that it will take two hours to cross it' (Wintersteller). Diemberger 'looks for a way to cross and tells us it will take two hours to pass the overhanging ice' (Schmuck). 'Kurt tries to cross the crevasse on the left and tells me he'll need two hours' (Buhl). At this Wintersteller got up, rammed his ice axe into the wall on the other side of the crevasse and stepped across. Schmuck followed him, using two ski poles and clearly much impressed with the audacity of the move. In his diary Schmuck noted 'The Ice Specialist' though it is not clear whether this is a disparaging remark about Diemberger, a comment on the impressive climb of Wintersteller or on his own crossing which was rather less impressive.

Beyond the crevasse Schmuck and Wintersteller again shared the task of trail breaking, but the steeper ground was more exhausting. Below the crevasse the leader had been able to make 50 steps before having to step aside, but now it was down to 20 or 30. Having stepped aside the resting climber waited until the trailmaker had made ten or so steps, then started after him, the easier job of following meaning he caught the leader just as he was stepping aside to rest. Schmuck says that the two of them made increasingly less subtle hints about the need for assistance, but Buhl and Diemberger both declined to take turns, each claiming to be exhausted. Finally Schmuck and Wintersteller were also exhausted and paused for a rest. Just below them the other two stopped and removed their rucsacs in the hope of being able to continue the climb unencumbered. Again Schmuck asked them to take the lead, but again they refused (though it is clear from Schmuck's diary that it was only Diemberger who declined) and 'after excuses like they have not had enough to eat, not enough sleep and have over-exerted themselves in the past few days (but what about the coolies Fritz and Marcus?) we take their condition on board. We let them have everything that they can eat from our rucsacs, even though these are our provisions for the summit! We then take off our rucsacs too and climb the ever steeper slope towards the Wind Gap. Hermann once again contributes to the murderously arduous task of track laying, each of us doing 30 steps at a time, while Kurt, totally apathetic, follows in our tracks' (Schmuck). Buhl's account is similar: 'It is past midday and we have to hurry, so we leave our rucsacs and start up the last very long and steep face. Fritz, Markus and I take turns laying tracks. Kurt stays at back, he's had it and is apparently no longer up to laying tracks. I too find it very difficult, the others likewise, and the three of us take turns every 10m.'

The expedition now hit a crisis as Buhl told Schmuck that 'he is in a bad way and wants to give up and go back. My encouraging words dissuade him for the moment. Come on, Hermann, have a drink. Kurt meanwhile has passed me. In answer to my request to hack some steps into the ice I just hear "I can't go on, why don't you do it!?"' The steps Schmuck wanted cut were necessary because Wintersteller, climbing out ahead, had cramponed up the slope to the base of the last short rock wall to the Wind Gap. The wall turned out to be difficult, Grade 4 rock overlaid with ice. When the others reached it Schmuck was concerned that Buhl and Diemberger, both exhausted, might not be able to get up it unaided. He therefore took the rope from Buhl and called to Wintersteller who descended to a point just above the crux of the short wall. Schmuck threw the rope and, eventually, Wintersteller caught it, climbed back up to the col, anchored it to a rock pinnacle and lowered it back down.

To the Forepeak

Wintersteller had now reached the Wind Gap and studied the ridge ahead. He shouted down encouragement to Buhl, telling him that it was not far now and that the ridge was climbable. Schmuck reached him first: next came Diemberger. 'Kurt comes up the rock wall. Still struggling to breathe he forces out words worthy of our life saver. "Fritz, thank you very much!" At my somewhat surprised look he repeats them – "yes really, thank you very much"'(Schmuck). Wintersteller also noted the acknowledgement in his diary: 'I secure the 20m rope to a rock pinnacle so that my companions have something to hold on to. Kurt thanks me effusively for this.'

Buhl's report showed his admiration for Fritz Wintersteller's climbing on the last section to the Wind Gap: 'Kurt is certainly the most shattered of us and he follows behind. I too am more than a little done in. I have overtaxed myself in the last few days, or was it hunger – there was too little breakfast today and I don't react well to that. The person in best shape is still Fritz and he therefore does most trailing. The last 100m to the Wind Gap is a steep ice slope. I have to admire how Fritz masters this slope, cutting steps in it. He also makes it up the last rocks with assurance and finally stands on the Wind Gap – perhaps 7900m high. Kurt follows very unsurely. It takes all his strength of will

Buhl and Diemberger at 8am on the 29 May during the first summit attempt. The two are at about 7300m.

to drag himself forward. Then Markus follows with a bit more assurance than before.'

From the west it is clear that the southernmost head of the 'triple-headed Breithorn of the Karakoram' comprises a high, saucer-shaped ridge, but it was not clear to the Austrians which end of the ridge was the highest. From the Wind Gap at a height of 7900m the Austrians could now see the long curving ridge once more, but again it was not clear which end of it was the actual high point of the mountain. While he waited for Buhl, Schmuck, re-asserting his leadership of the team, gave his approval to Wintersteller and Diemberger to start on the ridge to the peak at the northern end of the final ridge. They had to discover whether this was the true summit: time was moving on and the weather, so good early in the day, had now begun to deteriorate. Having sent the other two off, Schmuck waited for Buhl who was struggling up the fixed rope: 'I wait for Hermann. I want to continue together with him towards the goal for which we have striven so ardently. I wait for more than half an hour. The sun comes through from time to time and I take pictures of Fritz and Kurt as they, with Fritz always ahead, climb the slope to the peak. Hermann, exhausted, finally catches up and says "Don't think badly of me because of the state I'm in." That is out of the question. I've waited although I am in much better shape. We began this thing together and whatever the outcome may be, that's how I want it to finish. After 20 minutes I continue with Hermann. I walk slowly ahead of him, taking a few photos from time to time, partly because I want pictures of the middle peak and partly to allow Hermann time to recover a little.' It is diffi-cult not to have sympathy for Buhl and to marvel again at his iron resolve. Despite his condition and the pain from his dam-aged foot he was still moving forward, if now very slowly. It is also admirable that Schmuck decided to stay with his friend so that they would finish together the job they started.

Buhl's diary and report indicate the problems he was having. His diary begins at the base of the final rock wall to the Wind Gap: 'Fritz goes ahead, cutting a few steps. Kurt follows at his heels, no longer capable of cutting steps. Indeed, he has trouble staying upright. Markus has recovered a bit and climbs behind

Kurt. I'm not well. I am very sleepy and realise that it's getting too late. So I stay below and wait until they are all at the Wind Gap. This takes a long time, and then it is more time before the ropes are secured. By now it's between 4 and 5 in the evening and I urge them to turn back, but Kurt says I should come up as it's not much further to the peak. So I start climbing. Kurt, who had previously several times expressed the wish to reach the peak with me because Maix would have really liked that, is now up ahead with Fritz. Markus waits for me and the two of us follow them. The ridge is wonderful, a snow ridge with very steep flanks, great cornice and mushroom shapes, vertical pillars of snow to the north. The middle peak is even more fantastic.' Buhl's report is even more dramatic: 'Laying the tracks has done us all in, that and the severe cold. I am overcome by a terrible need to sleep and nearly fall asleep in the steps. Without protection the ice flank seems far too dangerous to me in these circumstances and so I stay below and watch. To be honest, I don't have much drive today and don't feel I have to reach the peak at all costs. I can understand how it is with the others, it would be their first 8000er. Now it is 5 o'clock and the other three are still trying to anchor a rope at the Wind Gap. I warn them that it is getting too late for the peak and that they should come down, but the only answer from above is that it's not much further and not difficult, and that I should come up. That persuades me. Things then do seem to be going better than I feared, with Fritz and Kurt already making their way along the ridge. Markus is waiting for me at the Wind Gap. I am surprised at what comes next. No rocks as one would have assumed: on the other side of the ridge there is a broad area of snow with fantastic snow formations, the like of which I know only from pictures of the north-east spur of Kangchenjunga, never having seen anything like them with my own eyes. Sharp cornices and enormous mushrooms of snow from which vertical ribs of snow with sharply defined edges descend into the abyss towards the north. Deep below a glacier stretches away with a surface like the skin of a crocodile. There are brown mountains bordered by white snowfields. At the same altitude as us, the bright white walls of Gasherbrum IV are illuminated. It's a fascinating scene, but it

Left to right: Wintersteller, Diemberger and Buhl rest below the crevasse which blocked the first attempt until Wintersteller negotiated it. The photograph was taken by Marcus Schmuck whose camera was failing to wind on correctly.

does not so inspire me that the going gets any easier. I drag myself along behind Markus. I don't know what's wrong with me, I just don't seem to have the right stuff today. Fifty metres above me Fritz and Kurt work their way up a very steep snow slope and make their way around an almost vertical snow wall in the rocks. Now and again I look back to the middle-peak – non plus ultra. Now there is a sharp ridge of rock, so steep that I ask myself how it even stays in place. Beyond, snow pillars descend into the abyss again, and from there, now and again, thick clouds of fog ascend. The weather seems worse to the north. Soon we too are swathed in fog. Markus and I are approximately at the height of the middle peak, about 8000m. Fritz and Kurt, perhaps 50m higher, have reached a point that from where we stand seems to be the summit. It is 6 in the evening and I call to them that they should turn back immediately, otherwise night will catch us and we have no bivouac equipment as our rucsacs are below the Wind Gap. They take my advice and we rush to get out of danger.'

In these accounts from Buhl there are indications that he was ill, as well as lacking motivation for the climb (though the two would likely be linked).

Ahead of Buhl and Schmuck, Wintersteller broke trail all the way to the top of the ridge, Diemberger following in his tracks. Wintersteller's delightful phrase when I asked whether Diemberger shared the lead on this last section of the ridge was that he had not, having chosen to 'graciously hold back'. Wintersteller went on to say that the ridge climb had been hard, sometimes six breaths for each step and a long pause after just three steps, and always with Diemberger 'trotting along behind'. He noted, with obvious satisfaction, that even though he was tiring Diemberger was barely able to keep up with him. But Wintersteller was tiring – finally, even the strong man was having problems, Schmuck noticing that 'Fritz is able to work his way up, but only with what is left of his strength as I can tell from the way he is climbing and using the ice axe to pull himself up. Kurt just crawls after him.' As the exhausted Wintersteller reached the 'top' the weather closed in, shutting off the view. In his book Diemberger states that from the Forepeak (as the rise at the northern end of the summit ridge is now called) he and Wintersteller could see the main summit and knew it was higher. But the diaries of both Schmuck and Wintersteller state that fog-like cloud prevented them from seeing whether this was the case and that the decision to return to the mountain was based on the need to clear up the uncertainty. Though less emphatic, Buhl's accounts support this.

When the lead pair reached the Forepeak it was 6.30pm and snow had begun to fall, adding to the difficulties that the fog would cause them on the descent. Wintersteller hastily built a cairn of stones and climbed back down, passing Schmuck and Buhl on his way to the Wind Gap. Quickly descending the fixed rope Wintersteller decided against waiting for the others – he had done enough today – and started to slide back down to Camp 3. He arrived at 8.15pm, an astonishing performance, one which he attributes to a descent mostly on the seat of his trousers, but one which was not without incident. At one point his slide went out of control and he somersaulted down the slope, losing his ice axe and gloves. Far enough behind for darkness to overcome them, which put an end to the chances of sliding, the other three were also having an epic.

'We turn towards the Wind Gap. The rocky parts on the way to it are a considerable challenge. I even give up breathing through my nose, which I had been doing during the ascent to lessen the strain on my throat. A rapid descent was critical so I decided this was OK.' Schmuck had been trying to breathe exclusively through his nose to avoid high-altitude cough which he knew to be debilitating. Now, in extremis, he allowed himself the luxury of breathing through his mouth!

'Fritz uses the rope from the Wind Gap first, I'm the last: Hermann and Kurt start down at 19.30, then I leave the Wind Gap. I make my way down the rope concentrating hard. I leave the rope hanging there because one thing's for sure, we'll come back in order to find out if this was the summit or not, to take pictures of it and perhaps have a go at the middle peak. Fritz is long gone now. I catch up with Hermann and Kurt. This can't be called "trudging downwards" anymore, it is more like falling and constantly picking yourself up again before collapsing. Breathing is like a constant gasping for air. We go down, falling, picking ourselves up again, sliding on the steep snow slope. We are racing against the oncoming darkness. Hermann rushes on in Fritz's tracks but I have to keep waiting for Kurt. Finally I surrender to temptation, sit on my bottom and slide down – how pleasant – after the dark form of Hermann. Suddenly I don't feel snow anymore but ice! With an almost subliminal sense of great danger I raise myself, turn around and can only just manage to stop myself with my ice axe. Beneath me an ice wall of at least 50m, above me Hermann, still following Fritz's tracks downwards. Then Fritz's track also disappears, Hermann finding the track again 15m further down. I learned the same evening how Fritz descended this section – a fall with several somersaults, in the process of which he lost his ice axe and gloves. We cross to the cone of sheer ice above Camp 3. We were now very worried about Fritz. A fall here would have been one of about 1500m. We are still looking for Camp 3 … and it has long since become dark. We call out, the calls echoing through the cold, starry night. Fritz! Camp 3! Hermann has taken a lower route while I've stayed further up and to the left as I am fearful of another ascent because I could hardly have managed one. Deep below I hear Hermann and Kurt shouting, but their calls die away. Has something happened to them? No – but there is no response to our calls. Left and right over the ice ridge we wearily descend. Then far below I see a light in a tent. At first I don't ask what it is as I am afraid that it is Base Camp 2200m below. But that's impossible I tell myself and only then do I dare to head straight towards it. What strange thoughts. After 20 minutes I reach Camp 3. Kurt is right behind me. Fritz lies motionless, fully clothed in his sleeping bag. Hermann is about to do the same. Without saying anything I too am soon tucked up in my sleeping bag.'

Buhl adds a very personal note to the descent: 'I can barely see my hand in front of my face. An icy wind blows along the whole slope, whipping my already ice-crusted face with needles of ice. My nose burns like fire because it has been exposed alternately to sun and cold, and a centimetre-long icicle hangs from it. My lips are cracked and hurt, my beard rustles with ice crystals, and my eyes hurt from trying to make things out in the darkness ... Now I see candlelight from Fritz's tent. ... It's gone 10 at night. I send a beam from my torch up a couple of times so that the others can orientate themselves, then that's it, into the sleeping bag. A quarter of an hour later Markus, and then Kurt, arrive. Neither says anything or has anything to eat. Why try anyway? Everything is frozen. I just head for my sleeping bag, where I sink into a dreamless, narcotic sleep.'

Down to Base Camp

On 30 May Wintersteller wrote that they had all resolved to return to the mountain, echoing Schmuck's remark that they had to take photos to prove that they were there as well as checking to see if the top at the far end of the ridge was higher. Wintersteller then noted: 'Marcus waited for Hermann, his climbing-partner, at the Wind Gap. Hermann is definitely still suffering from the after effects of his diarrhoea and sickness.

Another photograph from Schmuck's failing camera. This one shows Wintersteller, Diemberger and Buhl approaching the last steep section below Broad Col.

Kurt, without his ski-poles, armed solely with his ice axe, hardly laid any tracks all day, but he reached the top. A great injustice? Whatever, he was, after all, the smart one.'

Wintersteller's description of the descent from Camp 3 is laconic, noting merely that Schmuck left at 1pm, he following at 2pm. He reached Camp 2 at 3pm, Buhl and Diemberger arriving at 5pm. Sick and exhausted they decided to stay the night at the camp. Buhl's diary suggests that the decision to stay was actually forced on them because of Diemberger's condition: 'Wake up at 11. Sunshine on the tent, but the wind is blowing. Beautiful weather, but very cold. I still feel the effects of the previous day. Kurt seems as good as dead. He is motionless. At midday Fritz and Markus descend to Camp II and it takes all my effort to get Kurt to his feet by 4 o'clock. He is terribly lethargic and left alone would probably not leave his sleeping bag again. Everything is frozen, we can't eat anything. At 4 we leave Camp III. We leave most of the stuff in the tents, including all my photo equipment as we'll be back soon. Very strenuous descent, but safe thanks to the fixed ropes. We arrive at Camp II at 4.30. Fritz and Markus want to descend to Base Camp immediately in order to have a proper rest. They have prepared tea for us. It's great to have a hot drink, the first for two days. Kurt won't hear of descending, so we stay here. We find some fuel and get the Primus going. After a long time we have a pot of hot water with juice and have warmed up some food. It was really my initiative, even though Kurt took over and completed the job. However, two days later at Base Camp he declares that I had him to thank for the meal.'

Wintersteller and Schmuck did indeed descend, reaching Base Camp that evening to be met by Qader with coffee and a meal of meat and cabbage. Of the descent Wintersteller had little to say in his dairy. By contrast Schmuck's description of the descent went into great detail, just as he had for the descent from the Forepeak. 'I awake from a deep sleep at 9am. The sleeping bag is covered with snow and frost. Indescribable thirst. I put our plastic flasks, the drinks now frozen, into my sleeping bag in order to obtain a few drops of liquid. These taste good, but are dangerously cold! We turn round wearily in our sleeping bags from time to time muttering a few words. What eventually becomes clear to us is that we have to go down because our condition will hardly improve up here without warm food and drink. It's not until 1.30pm that I can persuade myself to leave. Fritz, with whom I am sharing the tent, also gets ready. In the neighbouring tent they are also packing things for the descent. The steep scree slopes are frozen into ice humps. Propped on my ski poles I go down to where the ropes have been fixed to secure our descent. I let myself down the sheer ice on the ropes having tied the ski poles to my rucsac and put on my crampons. The rope has frozen to the slope and I have to rip it out of the ice, which costs me the last ounce of my strength. I can rip 10m of it loose in one attempt, then this test of strength is required again. To be on the safe side I have wrapped the rope once around my arm and several times I bend my knees, turn my head to the ice, press my front points in and hold the weight of my body secure with the rope around my arm. For seconds I close my eyes, my lungs working hard, then I force myself down this fearful icy stretch to the Herrligkoffer depot at the lower end of the Ice Chapel. I collapse there. Whistling fragments of ice and rock tell me to be careful and to hurry away from this place. I hear Fritz 200m above me coming down, coughing. I manage to make the last 150m down to the plateau, coughing myself. With a final effort I continue across the almost flat part of the plateau. I want to lie down, to go no further, but it is only a few more metres to Camp 2 under the cornice. As I descend the cornice I see that a great chunk of it next to our camp has disappeared into the depths. The thought of the camp having gone is fearful. It is our last hope. There! It's still standing! Although the ski pole which served to secure one of the tents is shattered everything is still standing! I sink to my knees, fall sideways onto my rucsac and am lost in thought. With difficulty I take off the rucsac, crawl to the cooker, turn it on and start to melt snow while I take out my water flask to quench my thirst, adding sugar to strengthen myself a little. The sun rises slowly over the cornice. Warming, consoling, it shines down on our yellow and orange tent. Gradually the sun warms me and brings my strength back. Fritz arrives 20 minutes later descending careful-

Hermann Buhl at Broad Col. Another shot taken with Schmuck's faulty camera.

ly from the plateau. His silence speaks volumes. I offer him tea which he drinks lying in our tent, savouring it thankfully. I prepare several litres of tea. Still weakened we sit in front of our camp and consider our supplies. We decide that it is impossible for us to fully recover with what we have here, and decide we must descend to Base Camp this very day. I make tea for Hermann and Kurt and put it in the thermos. At 17.00 Fritz and I want to descend: we have already had great difficulty putting on our crampons. Here comes Hermann, and then Kurt too. They seem to be in even worse shape than we are. They accept the tea thankfully. It is savoured wordlessly at first. Kurt's face and the area around his mouth are particularly badly affected. With his head hung low he sits on the snow bench in front of the tent. We tell them that we intend to descend. We want to stick to our plan no matter what, although it is already late. However, they want to stay here – it was the right decision, they probably wouldn't have made it to Base Camp. Using one ski pole and an ice axe, with mixed feelings we descend the 50° slope. Will the slope hold or not? It does. I could never have believed that the descent would be such an effort. We fight to take in air while hurrying down the rugged, steep glacier because it is now very late. Often we sink in above the knee and we allow ourselves to rest on our backs for a few seconds before continuing. After leaving the steep glacier our tracks lead sideways down to Camp 1 via a 40° snow flank. Fritz sits on his bottom and slides. I watch him, horrified – does he have the strength to stop himself safely at the right time with his ice axe? I would hardly have that kind of strength anymore. He stops safely at the same altitude as Camp 1. I walk and arrive there minutes later. We try to make radio contact with Base Camp so that Qader can prepare food and drink, which he most kindly does whenever we are in need of it and we are too tired to do it ourselves, but our attempt is in vain. It is now 18.10 and we continue descending. On the huge, 40° snow slope Fritz sits down again and slides. It is rough frozen snow and I walk. It seems simply too dangerous to me but the sheer effort of walking tempts me to slide too. It goes very well, I can stop myself easily. After overcoming my fear of this same 200m long slope I follow in Fritz's tracks without inci-

113

dent and, most importantly, without effort. At the bottom where the gully is only 2m wide and becomes steeper, about 50°, we have to be careful because a slip would mean sliding down a 300m long system of channels, swinging to and fro and constantly hitting the side walls, and ending up on the 200m-high steep avalanche cone that leads down to the Godwin-Austen (Glacier). Treading carefully at first, then sliding we arrive safely at the glacier. At last the danger lies behind us. On the moraine we take off our crampons and shake our boots and trousers free of snow, then walk towards Base Camp using ski poles for support. We must first cross the glacier in order to get to the middle moraine. Unsteady on our feet we start out as if walking on dry land after weeks on board ship. Climbing between the ice towers, even if it is only 15m–20m, is murderous. Resting we look back again at Broad Peak which is still gleaming in the sunlight – if only we were on the peak today, no clouds, no snowfall! Was it really the peak we were on that now shines down on us so regally at 19.30!? We don't know exactly, so we pull ourselves together and continue through the ice towers to reach the moraine. I go ahead in the twilight, again and again sinking into the snow. Behind us K2 is luminously white. We stop from time to time, breathing with difficulty. We call out hoping those at the camp will know we are coming. When we begin the short ascent to the camp, a light goes on in Qader's tent and there he is. We put down our rucsacs, the ski poles are rammed into the ground behind the tent and then we sit in the kitchen tent telling our story while Qader provides us with meat and cabbage, with beer, tea and coffee. Tired. In bed 22.00. Deep sleep, dreaming.'

As a description of the sheer effort of moving at high altitude, especially when exhausted, this could hardly be improved. In about 40 hours the two men had climbed up 900m, then down 3000m.

At Base Camp on 31 May Schmuck and Wintersteller breakfasted on fresh eggs, biscuits, honey, and tea. They rested and worried about the other two: had they the strength to descend? Would the condition of the mountain allow them safe passage?

Would the two at Base Camp have the personal resources to mount a rescue? With visibility limited by the weather, there was little they could do immediately, so Schmuck worried about the state of their own health. Wintersteller's face and lips were ravaged by cold and sun and both men had spongy fingertips, an early sign of frostbite. Schmuck was also concerned about the state of his big toes. To ward off incipient frostbite they tried the then-accepted, now discounted, remedy of alternate hot and cold, plunging their extremities into hot water and then into the snow.

Finally at 1.30pm Buhl and Diemberger arrived. Below Camp 2 a huge windslab avalanche, probably caused by part of the cornice above the camp collapsing, had swept the slope that the route crossed. As Wintersteller, the realist, noted, at least now the slope would probably be safe for their return. Schmuck wrote that the two arrivals were silent, Diemberger's head was hanging down and his throat and tongue were so raw he could hardly swallow the tea and food he was offered. Schmuck wondered about Diemberger lack of emotion – was he really so phlegmatic, or was he absolutely exhausted? Schmuck concluded that it was probably a bit of both.

Buhl told the others of his struggle to get Diemberger down, a struggle he also noted in his account of the descent: 'Up at 8. Weather worse. Descend at 9.30 without breakfast. Tent shovelled free again on its right side. The cornice had broken off days before but has not harmed the camp. The steep flank beneath camp has broken off as a big windslab. I don't like having that cornice above camp any more. A lot of stuff stays at Camp II. Argument with Kurt, because despite being urged to take part in the shovelling, he immediately puts on his crampons, explaining that he has had it. Really have to push him so he carries on. Very strenuous descent. At 12 on Godwin-Austen Glacier. There have been big changes here, less snow, the ice towers are even more bizarre and already there are several small glacial lakes. It is very humid. At 1 in Base Camp. Drank, ate and slept a lot. Kurt still just as apathetic, he hasn't laughed for days – as if he has been castrated. He is starting to get on my nerves. In the evening I have a big argument with Kurt because of his neglect of his duties, of comradeship etc. Kurt still eats excessively, despite many warnings, and pays no attention to the rest of us. Kadar [sic] has fallen out with him too, because Kurt is always asking him to do the washing up. He is our accompanying officer not our cleaning maid. Kurt often has a provocative manner. The only positive attribute he has is his singing. You mean the best by him but he just takes it the wrong way and as a result he can't accept anything. Only occasionally does he have lighter moments – when he can really do things on his own. He is still too young.'

Schmuck's diary continues very significantly, both for what he says about that same evening and for what he leaves out. He notes that 'nobody speaks of further aims, that is Hermann and Kurt of K2, Gasherbrum IV, Hidden Peak. Instead we content ourselves with the very nice idea of climbing Paiju Peak.' He goes on: 'camp life continues. Both (Buhl and Diemberger) go from the kitchen to the tents. It takes a long time for Kurt to bring himself to undress, while Hermann is in his sleeping bag straight away. In the evening we meet only for dinner. Everyone still very tired.' But Wintersteller's version of events is quite different: 'In the evening there is a loud argument between Hermann, Kurt and Marcus. Hermann reproaches Kurt for going to the top without him against their implicit agreement. Marcus points out to Kurt that he hasn't laid even a metre of track and has had an easy time at our expense. I remind them of our agreement at the beginning of the expedition – "It doesn't matter who gets to the top, the only important thing is that one of us does, though it would be ideal if we could all make it", and I ask them to stop arguing.'

Quite clearly something happened that evening, something which is reflected in Schmuck's diary over the next few days despite his never mentioning the argument. Conversations with Schmuck and Wintersteller, and also, but to a much lesser extent, with Diemberger, have shed light on the events, but before considering them it has to be remembered that at the time of the argument no one knew if Diemberger and Wintersteller had reached the real summit. It seems that the initial arguments

116

Hermann Buhl following the tracks of Wintersteller and Diemberger across Broad Col towards the Forepeak on 29 May 1957.
Wintersteller, ahead, and Diemberger can be seen on the climb to the Forepeak. To the left is the true summit of Broad Peak. To the right of the Forepeak is the rising cloud which soon obscured the view and so forced the Austrians to return eleven days later.

centred around Schmuck's accusation that Diemberger had done little to justify his having reached the top. Having not reached the top himself Schmuck was clearly annoyed at having missed out. Had Wintersteller reached the top alone Schmuck might have accepted it, but he felt cheated by Diemberger's success. Buhl then joined the argument against Diemberger, pointing out that the pair had an agreement to reach the top together and that Diemberger has reneged on it. If this is correct (and it is certainly implied by Buhl's suggestion that 'Maix would have really liked that') then it implies that the weakened Buhl, aware that he was unlikely to be able to keep up with Schmuck and Wintersteller, had come to an agreement with the other slow climber that they would stay together and help each other. Buhl's aggravation must have been heightened by the fact that Diemberger had not only broken the agreement, but also reached the top. The news that there was a special deal between Buhl and Diemberger further enraged Schmuck. He had waited at Broad Col for Buhl when he could have continued with Wintersteller. In conversation Wintersteller suggested that had Schmuck continued with him rather than waiting at the col they might have had the time to reach the true summit, though in view of the late hour and the deteriorating weather that is questionable. What is certainly true is that Buhl and Diemberger were unlikely to have made the Forepeak, and would certainly not have made the main summit. Although Schmuck's diary ignores the arguments, there seems little doubt that it was that evening's exchanges which finally split the expedition into two. If there was to be a second attempt on Broad Peak, and Schmuck, at least, was now absolutely adamant that there would be, he and Wintersteller would climb together. They were obviously the strongest of the four and they got on well. And neither seemed keen to be teamed with Buhl or Diemberger.

In his diary for the following day (1 June) Wintersteller noted that Buhl and Diemberger 'have become more modest, no more talking about K2, Gasherbrum II and Hidden Peak: they content themselves with Paiju Peak.' What is interesting is that his and Schmuck's diaries make similar comments a day apart, suggesting that they wrote up their daily logs at different times. Schmuck also had GIV rather than GII as Wintersteller writes: Buhl and Diemberger, the ambitious duo, had obviously been making tentative plans for all the peaks of the Gasherbrum massif. Wintersteller also noted more details from Buhl's account of the descent of the second pair, Buhl claiming that he had to pull Diemberger from his sleeping bag at Camp 3 and that had he not done so 'it would have been all over for him.' In conversation Wintersteller uses a rather more eloquent expression, suggesting that Buhl's view was that without his assistance Diemberger would have snuffed it. If Diemberger was so exhausted it is no surprise that the two had to spend a night at Camp 2.

At Base Camp 'it snowed overnight and it keeps snowing all day. In the last few days we have had incredible luck with the weather.' Wintersteller's comment is likely to have been correct. Had the bad weather arrived two days earlier and caught them all at Camp 3 the outcome might have been very different, as it might have been had it been just one day early and caught the more exhausted pairing at Camp 2. On 1 June Schmuck's diary is sparse: 'Rest day like we never had before, meaning we really could rest. We are still very tired. Strange how an advance into the 8000m zone can have such after-effects, although we have no other injuries. Kurt stands out because of his attitude!' Diemberger, it seems, is still smarting over the attacks a few days before.

Trying to smooth things over, on 2 June Schmuck made a significant effort to bring some harmony back to the team. His diary notes a special lunch he prepared, a lunch which came complete with a typed menu: 'I make an effort to put together a good menu for lunch:

<u>Broad Peak Menu</u>
Baltoro Soup à la Knorr
Hash Browns à la Pfanni
Askole Compote
Marcus Custard à la Haas
Glacier Water à la Meindl'

(Pfanni is the trade name for a type of potato dumpling.)

This went down well, but Schmuck then noted wearily that 'Hermann starts making nasty remarks again. Kurt just lets it wash over him.'

It seems a case could be made for Buhl being jealous of Diemberger, but if that is conjectured then it raises the question of why, and why only Diemberger. As far as reaching the top of the mountain was concerned Buhl's rivals were Schmuck and Wintersteller, particularly Wintersteller who had shown himself not only to be a competent climber (having led the most important and difficult pitch on the route) but also the strongest. Buhl seemed to have become resigned to the fact that he could not compete with these two, but was exerting influence over the younger man. Both Schmuck and Wintersteller maintain that Buhl would not allow Diemberger to lead when they were together (though this view is not supported by Buhl's diary). In considering the available material it seemed to me that a case could be made for Buhl seeing in Diemberger a younger version of himself. Though not as accomplished a climber as Buhl, Diemberger was fiercely ambitious, as his later career has shown. On the world stage Buhl's position was under threat. On the 1954 Italian K2 expedition the star was Walter Bonatti who, though he had not reached the summit, had survived a bivouac at 8000m after taking equipment up to the summit team. Born in 1930 Bonatti had risen to prominence with his ascent of the east face of the Grand Capucin in 1951. In 1955, he made an astonishing solo first ascent of the south-west pillar of the Petit Dru over five days, a climb which many were hailing as the greatest ever in the Alps. Was Buhl using Diemberger as a proxy for all those youngsters who were competing – even if they did not realise they were – for Buhl's position as the world's pre-eminent climber? When I suggested to Diemberger that Buhl might have been jealous of him he disagreed – but then he might not be the best judge. Diemberger thought that Buhl was certainly jealous of Wintersteller's strength and claimed that Wintersteller had exploited this occasionally in a show of one-upmanship. Diemberger said that if Buhl was trail making Wintersteller would occasionally make a separate trail, overtaking Buhl who, as might be expected, would then step into the made trail. As we have seen, Buhl mentions this in his diary. In conversation Wintersteller admitted there was an element of truth in this, but denied that he was in competition with Buhl. The fact was that he was stronger than Buhl and would follow his trail until he caught him. At that point, he says, it was to everyone's advantage that he continue ahead, pushing the route out. It is hard to disagree – so far Wintersteller's strength and his indomitable spirit had taken the Austrians to the Forepeak.

On the day of the Broad Peak Menu Wintersteller noted that 'Kurt makes breakfast and Qader shows himself even more to be a great guy. He even cooks for us as well as listening to the weather reports.' But Wintersteller too, though trying at all times to be even handed, had to add a rider, noting that though Qader was getting on well with the team, 'only with Kurt he has a problem, because Kurt is constantly bothering him with special demands.'

On that rest day (2 June) the weather was bad at first with a succession of avalanches thundering down the mountains, but then improved a little. Eventually the top section of Broad Peak became visible again, Buhl picking out Camp 3 with his binoculars. It was still there, which was a relief to them all as they had worried that the snow or avalanches might have destroyed it.

As the weather improved, so did the health of the Austrians, though Buhl's frost-nipped toes were giving him trouble. But relationships in the team were still strained. Wintersteller's diary details how he washed and dried his clothes, but then includes: 'At noon we sit over a pleasant meal and discuss recent events. Kurt alone takes no part in the conversation, instead he stuffs his face. The observant Hermann can't help noticing, and says "Kurt! You've had enough to eat, leave some for us, or we'll have to start rationing it".' Schmuck, too, though trying hard to avoid the tensions, cannot. After noting that cooking was now done on a rota and 'Kurt prepares an excellent breakfast, Hermann rice with meat for lunch and Fritz the dinner' goes on 'Hermann and Kurt have already begun discussing our future!! If we're lucky we can try Gasherbrum IV, Masherbrum, maybe K2. The Paiju Peak in any case, and one of the Trango Towers too. What do I think of this? Well, first they are lying on the floor, unable to do anything, and now, half-way recovered, they are already talking big!' However he was, despite his frustration, at least pleased with the recovery of the two: 'Anyway the main thing is that they are healthy! In the evening the two constant quarrellers sing together again. Even when singing they start to argue. It's quite entertaining – singing – arguing – singing. If Kurt did not have to be constantly called to order one would have to feel sorry for him, but he is the perfect means by which the constantly moaning Hermann can let off steam!'

With the weather preventing the team from heading back to Broad Peak, but their physical condition improving, food and the relief of boredom were the main pre-occupations. 'Hermann makes custard for breakfast. For lunch Marcus surprises us with sausage-meat dumplings, which he has managed to concoct out of rusk, dried egg and ata (wheat flour). In the evening I reciprocate by making plum dumplings. What are 35 dumplings to five hungry men! They disappear in no time, and everyone looks at me as if I might have something more up my sleeve. But I haven't and we have to make do with the leftovers from lunch, together with a large pot of tea and some rusk and cheese' (Wintersteller). Schmuck is less thrilled with his lunchtime effort: 'Midday dumplings with dark flour and rusk, much too much flour!' He also noted the main activities of the day: morning – 'We lie in our tents', afternoon 'we lie down again.' Buhl, Wintersteller noted, had another snipe at Diemberger: 'Hermann asks poor Kurt to wash his hands properly before attending to his duties as orderly.' Buhl did not mention this incident in his diary, but did note another which, as we shall see later, may be of significance: 'Kurt asks for diary because he wants to catch up on things from Skardu on. Although he had the most time for writing and I often urged him to, he never kept up.'

Finally, something had to be done and on 5 June Schmuck took Qader skiing while Wintersteller prepared the loads for the mountain. That night the wind picked up. Schmuck had storm-lashed his and Wintersteller's tent in the hope of a quiet night, but it was not to be, the howling wind allowing him little sleep. In the next tent Buhl and Diemberger also had hardly any sleep. Wintersteller fared better, but was deeply concerned that if the wind was as bad at Camp 3 the tents would be shredded. He wished that the team had dropped them and weighed them down with stones. On 6 June the weather was fine, the sun shining. The Austrians wanted to wait one more day because of the bad night and to give the mountain a chance to shed any remaining avalanches. So, instead of setting off they made a morning ski tour of the local glacier, enjoying the warmth of the sun and taking photographs. During the tour Schmuck and Wintersteller were impressed by two unnamed peaks above the Savoia Glacier. Both were above 7000m, but looked very climbable. Back at Base Camp Diemberger made scrambled eggs for lunch, then the four men relaxed for the rest of the day: tomorrow would be an early start. Schmuck and Wintersteller appeared, from their diaries, relaxed about this second attempt. Only Buhl expressed a concern, that the '7 days of plenty' would perhaps take its toll on their fitness.

Schmuck's alarm went off at 3.15am on 7 June. By 4.15am he and Wintersteller were ready to leave, but Buhl and Diemberger were still asleep. With Qader accompanying them for the initial part of the walk, the first two set off for the mountain, making good progress on frozen snow. By around 7.30am they had reached Tooth Camp, but beyond that conditions were poor, the two men sinking up to their hips in soft snow. Swapping lead frequently the two ploughed on, reaching Camp 2 beneath the cornice at noon. It took them 90 minutes to shovel snow away from the first tent, but to their relief it was intact. Fifteen minutes later Buhl and Diemberger arrived. They 'arrive quite exhausted, despite the fact that we did all the hard work laying the tracks. Now it is their turn to shovel their tent free.' Wintersteller's opinion of any suggestion he help with the digging is ringingly clear in that diary entry, but he did make lunch – meat and cabbage, and tea – having first carved out a platform for a kitchen. But here again Buhl's diary entry was less generous about the actions of the first pair: 'Fritz and Markus always ahead. They seem to do this on purpose so that they can note in their diaries that "we laid the tracks again!"' It is difficult to believe that such pyrrhic delight was the reason for Schmuck and Wintersteller expending the effort to break trail, particularly as the pair knew only too well how desperately draining the summit climb would be. In the afternoon the four tended to their feet and equipment, then relaxed. There was a light snowfall, but the weather looked hopeful for the next day.

It turned out to be a marvellous day. It had been agreed the day before that Buhl and Diemberger would lay trail, but even though Wintersteller made them breakfast (tea and porridge) there was no sign that they were interested in doing so and in exasperation he set off in the lead again. He and Schmuck changed leads and, eventually, the other two caught up. Diemberger now took over in front, but after 200m Wintersteller had had enough of the slow progress and resumed his role out in front, Buhl noting that 'Fritz is doing his own thing again'. Leaving the rest increasingly far behind Wintersteller stayed out in front all the way to Camp 3 which he was pleased to find intact. The tent floors were covered in ice: two cameras, forgotten in the hasty retreat, though snow covered, were fine. Wintersteller then cooked the meal, Buhl noting that when he (Wintersteller) warmed two tins 'Markus immediately complains that it isn't hot enough. This quickly turns into a serious quarrel with bitter complaints and harsh words.' Buhl implies that the quarrel is between Schmuck and Wintersteller and also that this is not the first time: 'Mood in the other camp, as always on such decisive days, is rather fragile' (perhaps to be expected given the circumstances of a pioneering climb with no back-up, and no worse than the mood in the Buhl/Diemberger 'camp': Buhl's use of 'other camp' is itself illuminating); but the quarrel soon spread. 'Marcus tells me that I just decide things and give orders but never do anything. So I shut up. Fritz says we need to get all this into the open and coaxes our argument into laughter in order to restore the peace' (Buhl). After cooking the meal Wintersteller started to prepare drinks for the next day but the fuel ran out after he had made only 5 litres. That quantity would have to last for the next two days – just one and a quarter litres per man, much less than the recommended amount. After a discussion about the dangers of this, the four decided that the weather was too good to miss and that they would make a summit bid the next day.

The evening was beautiful. Buhl described the view from the camp, first seeking out Nanga Parbat in a passage which throws a light on his view of his own position in the climbing world: '… I can see far into the distance. Nanga Parbat stands out clearly against the horizon once again. I can see the pre-peak, the Silver Saddle, the enormous south flank, and as I look my thoughts wander back to my time on a mountain which provided my first great Himalaya adventure. More than just an adventure, the fulfilment of a dream. And after what I have seen and experienced here, my climb of it seems all the more improbable to me. Yes, truly legendary.'

All four men were in their sleeping bags by about 7pm, Schmuck and Wintersteller entertained by the bickering ('the usual' as Schmuck puts it) in the next door tent. Buhl says that he and Diemberger actually attempted to sing, but without a guitar and in the thin air the attempt proved futile.

In his book account of the summit climb Diemberger ends this night before the summit climb with 'Tomorrow and tomorrow and tomorrow ...', an apparently sophisticated literary allusion. Was he aware when writing this that the soliloquy which Shakespeare has Macbeth speak is actually on the futility of life and ambition?

Another of Marcus Schmuck's photographs of Hermann Buhl. This one was taken on the slopes of the Forepeak. Behind Buhl is Broad Col and the rocky shoulder of Middle Peak.

5
The Summit

Buhl's diary says that he slept well, but was forced to get up (probably at around midnight, though he is not explicit) to relieve himself. The moon was bright and he thought the team should start immediately: 'I would most dearly love to leave now and I call into the neighbouring tent to see if they want to. No answer, so I go back to sleep.' In his report Buhl wondered if the lack of a reply meant Schmuck was not in the mood for an early start. More likely, it would seem, was that Schmuck was asleep, but Schmuck's diary says that there was an exchange between them in the night: 'During the night Hermann pesters me, asking if we shouldn't leave by moonlight. I say no because I think we will climb much faster in daylight and conserve our strength better.' Buhl continued his diary by saying that he woke again at 1am, then looked at his watch every fifteen minutes or so until 2.30am when he finally lit a candle.

Despite his assertion to the contrary, Buhl must have had no, or little, sleep that night. His condition for the summit climb is disputed. Schmuck and Wintersteller both claim that though he had now recovered from his diarrhoea and sickness, he was still weak: if that is the case lack of sleep would have further debilitated him. But Diemberger does not agree with the Schmuck–Wintersteller diagnosis. Though Buhl had suffered from what Diemberger eloquently calls 'thin shits', so have they all to an extent and Buhl was now recovered, he says.

Marcus Schmuck following Fritz Wintersteller towards the Forepeak on 9 June 1957. At the Col the black dots are Buhl and Diemberger resting before their climb.

Wintersteller also says that Buhl took Pervitin on the summit day. Pervitin is a methamphetamine: on Nanga Parbat it had squeezed the last energy reserves from Buhl during his descent from the summit, contributing to his survival. But as with all drugs its usefulness comes at a price. As a family methamphetamines alter the rational workings of the brain. On Nanga Parbat Buhl had hallucinated during his descent (though oxygen debt from the thin air can have a similar effect). The drug also suppresses appetite. There is nothing in Buhl's diary or report to suggest he either had diarrhoea or was suffering from its after-effects, or that he had taken Pervitin. It does note that he had an altitude cough: 'I suffer from coughing fits at nearly every movement.' What troubled him on summit day, says Diemberger, was the pain in the foot damaged on Nanga Parbat caused by the intense cold. It is clear that on 9 June Buhl had another bad day, but whether the cause was simply pain in his frostbitten foot or some other debilitating condition remains a mystery.

But whatever his condition on the climb, as summit day dawned Buhl had a more immediate problem, his attempt to light a candle filling the tent with smoke and causing him to have another coughing fit.

Schmuck made no mention of being woken by Buhl at 2.30am, his diary starting with the lighting of a candle at 3.15am. He continued: 'We lie in our sleeping bags fully dressed because every move requires effort and will-power. We stay in our bags to eat the porridge with Ovaltine we prepared earlier – it provides only a hint of warmth – and drink the lukewarm tea. With great will-power we then leave our bags, which are covered with snow because the wind has torn open our tent. Wind-resistant trousers and overshoes are put on while we are still in the tent, but then we have to open the entrance. A wave of cold sweeps over me. The temperature is -30°C, but we have to put on our crampons without gloves.' Despite the cold, conditions are excellent: 'Not a cloud in the sky. Things couldn't have been better, and on top of that there is no wind when we leave Camp 3 at 4am' (Wintersteller).

From Schmuck's diary it seems that Schmuck and Wintersteller left first, shrouded against the bitter cold.

Schmuck emerging on to the Forepeak on 9 June.

Schmuck was concerned for his feet: 'Fritz closes our tent. With a ski pole and ice axe we ascend the slightly snow-covered ice hump. Soon, despite horsehair socks, wool socks, felt liners, boots and overboots, we can feel the cold in our toes.' The two pairs took different routes – 'Hermann and Kurt choose a steeper way more to the right, in order to avoid the crevasse that Kurt fears' (Wintersteller). Diemberger acknowledges this change of route and also notes that he and Buhl made slightly quicker progress on their more direct line, his book account noting that as the sun reached them they paused to take off their boots and rub their feet, at which point Schmuck and Wintersteller joined them. The latter pair had already paused to attend to their feet: 'At 8.30 Marcus and I rest under the crevasse at a height of 7500m. We rub our toes warm in the sunshine. It has taken us two hours less than on the 29 May. Some metres beyond the crevasse we meet our companions, who are still trying to warm their feet.'

Schmuck contemplating the climb along the final summit ridge from a point beyond the Forepeak.

In his diary Buhl agreed with much of what is in these accounts: 'The food thermos with the porridge is in the neighbouring tent. We have to wait until they have done with it and then we get our share. Meanwhile they are both ready and Markus goes ahead as usual, then Fritz follows and a quarter of an hour later it's our turn. It's 3.30am, -20°C outside the tent, windless, clear. The snow is hard at first, up to about 7300m, then it becomes looser. Only then do we reach the other two and in spite of cold feet I walk ahead and continue laying tracks, at first still in the old blown-over tracks, then, as agreed the day before, to the right. I go my way with Kurt behind me. In places the snow is very hard, but in other places I sink deeply into it. It is bitterly cold, maybe -30°C and I can't feel my right foot anymore. At 8 we come into the sun, beneath the steep flank at 7600m and [Fritz] and Markus come behind us in their own track. [In his report Buhl notes that 'Fritz and Markus climb in their own tracks – how stupid at this altitude – and moan that their route was no good at all.'] They have to admit that it was-

130

n't easy there either. We have a bite, take off our boots, and massage our feet, especially me, because I am suffering from a bit of frostbite on my right foot again. After half an hour, while I am still vigorously massaging my feet, Markus and Fritz get ready and continue climbing, though Fritz says we should keep massaging as the peak isn't worth the loss of a foot.'

There is no substantial difference between the accounts. Schmuck and Wintersteller start first, Buhl and Diemberger catch them as they are climbing in the trail prepared by the first pair. Buhl goes in front (not acknowledged by Schmuck and Wintersteller), but then takes a different line. Buhl's claim that this had been agreed the day before is disputed by both Schmuck and Wintersteller who are adamant that Buhl and Diemberger changed routes because they did not want to cross the crevasse which caused problems on the first attempt. But though the diary accounts are much the same, when Buhl typed his report he made a very significant change, noting 'Above the rocks near Camp III the dark silhouettes of Markus and Fritz stand out. Actually I'm a bit peeved because we had agreed to go together, but Markus and Fritz always do this, they never wait, simply taking off. Normally this doesn't really matter, but at 7000m and more it is difficult to make up even a quarter of an hour in time.' The difference is startling.

The report account was used in the Höfler/Messner book and, not surprisingly, annoyed Schmuck and Wintersteller, so much so that Wintersteller wrote to Höfler querying the provenance of the passage. Wintersteller's point was that at altitude following someone making a trail is much easier than making one, a direct contradiction of Buhl's report. As noted earlier, Schmuck and Wintersteller state that if the lead man was making, say, 20 steps before giving way to the second, the second would wait until the leader had made ten, then start, following being so much easier that the two would arrive at the 20th step together. To make up fifteen minutes when behind trailblazers would have been straightforward and Buhl's diary clearly states that he and Diemberger did indeed catch the first pair quite quickly. His report comment that Schmuck and Wintersteller were stupid to make their own trail below the crevasse reinforces the fact that following is easier than leading, Buhl contradicting his own comment. Buhl's report is a puzzle – why would he make such a claim? Was he retrospectively justifying his own slow pace? In practice he and Diemberger followed a made trail for the rest of the day and, far from being upset about it, were almost certainly overjoyed to be able to.

By the time the pairs met up Buhl was having trouble with his right foot, his Nanga Parbat frostbite amputations hurting him terribly in the cold, though his left foot seems to have been no more affected than the feet of the others. While Buhl and Diemberger massaged their feet, Schmuck and Wintersteller continued in the lead, a position they say they did not relinquish all day, though in his report Buhl claims that he and Diemberger caught them again below the Wind Gap and that he (Buhl) actually made trail for a while: given the timings admitted in all accounts – the second pair arriving at least 45 minutes, and perhaps 75 minutes, later at the Wind Gap – this seems very unlikely. It was already 11am, the cold, with the consequent constant need to swing their legs to get the circulation going, and the long pause to rub their feet, having eaten into the day. Schmuck was the first to leave: 'I began laying tracks on the flank of the Wind Gap. Fritz followed. We take turns: each of us laid the track for the next 40 steps upwards, then stepped aside, rammed his ice axe in and with closed eyes sank down on his knees, trying to calm his overworked lungs and to recover a little. When Fritz hesitantly passed me I followed the track behind him like a machine. It is a great relief not to be breaking in up to your calves with every step.' Occasionally, though, the advantage of not breaking trail was lost: '… suddenly I realise I am not breaking through the snow but standing on sheer ice and have to prevent myself from slipping down into the abyss.'

The pair were grateful for the rope left on the first attempt and hauling themselves up it they reached the Wind Gap: 'Crawling I reach the Wind Gap, turn around and sit, head propped on my knees hearing only my own quick breathing. It is 12.45. We both lie in the snow and wait for Hermann and Kurt in order to continue the attempt at the peak together.' But Buhl and Diemberger were going very slowly, despite the trail made by the first pair. Schmuck claims that it was not until 2pm that Diemberger arrives, though Diemberger says it was 1.30. (Buhl's diary actually states that Schmuck and Wintersteller had already left the Wind Gap before he and Diemberger arrived at 1.30, casting even more doubt on the likelihood that Buhl did any trail making between the crevasse and the col.) Whichever is correct, and it hardly matters, the lead pair had a decision to make: 'Fritz and I decide, considering how time is getting on, to continue the murderously arduous track-laying from here too.'

At the Wind Gap Buhl's diary says: 'I feel terrible, maybe from the cold, perhaps hunger as I have no appetite. Kurt mixes fruit, Pez [a type of sweet] and hazelnuts, and a gulp of tea, which I swallow reluctantly. I lie there and rest till 2.30, then we continue.' Buhl's report expanded on his condition: 'I am overwhelmed by a weariness that in normal circumstances I would call post-prandial tiredness. I lie down and would love to go to sleep. Kurt wants to give me various things to eat – sweets, dried fruit, hazelnuts – but nothing appeals and I have to force myself to swallow something. Not even a swig from the bottle appeals to me. Fritz and Markus keep their lead and are already moving along the ridge, that is, mostly Fritz ahead with Markus trailing behind him like a faithful dog. But the sight of them doesn't move me at all. I want to rest for a bit. It's going terribly slowly up there too, I think to myself, surely they don't feel as if they are on a country walk either.'

Ahead the first pair were indeed making slow, but steady progress: 'We slowly approach the peak that Fritz and Kurt reached eleven days ago. Is this the peak or not? This question constantly weighs on our minds as we climb. We come to a difficult rocky stretch on the ridge, a short chimney where we labour with hands, feet and body in order to drag ourselves up. After this I'm back in the snow and have to allow my breathing to recover. It's 3pm, time is racing on while we are gaining height only very slowly ... 10m still separates us from the place reached on 29 May. With a last effort of will I reach the small stone cairn that Fritz erected. I'm not very pleased when I realise that further along (the ridge) there is a higher peak' (Schmuck). As Wintersteller noted in his more objective style: 'we reach the pre-peak, where we turned back on 29 May. This time the view is clear – 400m away there is another, higher, peak which can easily be reached by walking along a partly snow-covered ridge.' It was about 4pm when the pair finally reached the Forepeak.

Schmuck then took up the story of the climb along that final, connecting ridge – 'After a short rest we begin to tackle the ups and downs of the ridge leading to the main peak. Time is of the essence now – we are already in the thirteenth hour of our ascent. I trudge along the western side of the ridge. The eastern side falls away vertically about 1500m.' In his book on the climb Schmuck added what he must have recalled later as it is not in his diary, that he was constantly telling himself to keep away from the cornices that overhung the precipitous eastern side of the ridge. The ridge was, though, a 'gentle stroll' after the rigours of the climb to the Forepeak.

Schmuck's diary continues: 'The last stretch before the summit is now ahead of us. The summit itself is a huge cornice. We stand 20m below on the last rock. Awed and happy for a moment we just stand there. Then each of us invites the other to begin the last steps to the top. Finally we do it together. It was 5.05pm when we stood on top of the huge cornice of Broad Peak's main, 8047m-high, peak. A wordless handshake was all we were capable of.' Again there is an addition in his book, Schmuck claiming that he did in fact have enough breath to utter a few words, managing an Austrian expression of surprise and joy which is best translated as 'Blimey Fritz – fantastic.'

On the summit: 'It requires a great effort to take the essential pictures. Our flags are taken from the rucsac, fastened to the ice axes and photographed. This sounds like a simple task, but to take off your gloves, baring your hands to the cold, opening the rucsac, fastening the flags to the ice axe, operating the camera and packing everything up again, costs us a lot of what little strength we have left. My camera isn't working anymore, but Fritz's Leica works as well as ever and so it is possible to record the moment in black and white as well as in colour.' (In fact Wintersteller had two Leicas, one loaded with colour film, the other with black and white.) In his diary Wintersteller added a

Fritz Wintersteller and Marcus Schmuck on the summit of Broad Peak, 5.05pm 9 June 1957. The shot was taken with a time release, Wintersteller having mounted his camera on a snow cairn.

little to the summit exploits: 'At 5.05pm Marcus and I hug each other in joy on the main peak. In the following hour we take pictures, for one of which I even build a snow cairn so I can take a picture using the delay-timer.'

There may have been little breath for talking and the effort of taking photos was extreme, but there was still time to admire the view, though the admiration was tempered by the knowl-

(Above) Marcus Schmuck on the summit. On this shot Schmuck
claims Diemberger and Buhl can be seen near the Forepeak – see
below.

(Above right) From the position at which Diemberger and Buhl separated they could see the summit and the lead climbers reaching it.
Schmuck claims that in the above photograph – one of the several of
him on the summit taken by Wintersteller – the second pair can be
seen close to the Forepeak, though Wintersteller is not convinced. In
this enlarged, enhanced section of the shot what appear to be
Diemberger, left, and Buhl, have been ringed.

edge that the beauty was a savage beauty: 'The sun is already worryingly low in the sky and a long descent awaits us. First a long ridge which partly involves ascending again, then an 1100m descent of snow and ice flanks to Camp 3. We have very little time to look around at the sea of Karakoram peaks between Tibetan Sinkiang and Pakistan which are bathed in the late sun. To the north K2 – which was conquered by a large Italian expedition at enormous expense – to the east the lower mountains of Sinkiang. To the south-east and south the 8000ers of Gasherbrum [Schmuck means Gasherbrum II] and Hidden Peak. Further to the south-west the proud pyramid of Masherbrum. Below us the Baltoro Glacier flows like a giant river, bordered far to the west by the impressive form of Paiju

137

Peak. 200km further west the massive form of Nanga Parbat is unmistakable. To the north among innumerable peaks I pick out the bold figure of the Mustagh Tower' (Schmuck). Schmuck also wonders where their team-mates are: 'So what's going on with our fellow-climbers, we all wanted to stand on top of the mountain. At the pre-peak we can distinguish a figure beginning to move towards us on the ridge.' In his book Schmuck elaborated on his summit stay, adding the detail that his oxygen-starved body seemed to be reacting so slowly to thoughts that he took to speaking to himself aloud, telling himself what to do – take off gloves, open rucsac, take out camera – because if he didn't then nothing actually happened. He also says that he was very concerned that Buhl and Diemberger might not make the summit because of exhaustion and the cold.

Wintersteller noted that he and Schmuck 'leave the summit at 5.50pm and shortly after meet Kurt coming up towards us, and, 25 minutes later, Hermann, who has already passed the pre-peak and the subsequent steeper part of the ridge.' Schmuck added little to this in his diary, but did in his book. There he wrote that Diemberger told him that Buhl had a lot of pain in his frostbitten foot and so was moving slowly, but that he was still moving and that he intended to continue to the top. Schmuck noted: 'that sounds like our Hermann'. In his diary Schmuck then recalls turning around to watch Diemberger as he reached the summit and 'to my horror' saw the younger man go past the end of the trail he and Wintersteller had made, out on to the cornice. This was, he says, 'sheer lunacy', but perhaps to be expected from Diemberger who is the 'baby' of the team and probably did not realise how dangerous his actions were.

Schmuck next recalled the meeting with Buhl on the ridge before the Forepeak. Buhl was in a bad way, but he was not going to stop. Schmuck knew Buhl too well to try to persuade him otherwise. It was, he says, 'another illustration of Buhl's extraordinary willpower, something that was almost incomprehensible in ordinary human terms. He would go to the top so that the whole team had succeeded, the first time that an entire expedition had reached the top on an 8000m peak on the same day. And without using oxygen and porters on the mountain.'

Fritz Wintersteller on the summit with K2 behind him.

Schmuck on the summit, this time with the Gasherbrum peaks behind him.

At the Wind Gap after a long rest Buhl and Diemberger had set off again, but their progress was slow, Diemberger noting that the distance they travelled between rests grew shorter and shorter. Buhl's account agrees. In his diary he stated: 'With effort I drag myself terribly slowly up the ridge behind Kurt. At the shoulder beneath the pre-peak it is 4.30 and Kurt, who believes that going on like this we can no longer reach the summit, asks me if he can continue on his own. I let him go. I sit down, wanting to wait – it's 5 o'clock and I see two dots at the summit very far away. It's Fritz and Markus. I also see how quickly Kurt manages the flank to the pre-peak and so I continue.' Buhl's report added to this: 'Kurt is going well now, strangely, as he wasn't in very good shape this morning. He goes ahead and I'm not unwilling to be dragged along by him, a bit like cyclists can be, but we are making slow progress. At 4.30 we have reached a point just beneath the pre-peak. There Kurt asks me, "Hermann, do you mind if I go ahead otherwise I won't make it to the summit". I recognise that in this condition I'm a burden to him and have nothing against his idea. This keen youngster is not going to miss out on an 8000er just because of me. I must honestly confess that I no longer have any particular ambition because my 8000er is Nanga Parbat and what I experienced there can't be repeated. I sit down, intending to wait until the others return from the top. Up there the first two have reached it, a narrow snowy summit on which I can see two small dots. My feet are troubling me again, they have gone dead. But then I notice how quickly Kurt manages the last stretch to the pre-peak. This inspires me and I say to myself, didn't we all, the whole team, want to get to the top? It is certainly very late, gone 5. Is there still enough time? I'll try it. At least I'll have the moon as an escort.'

This account of the parting of Buhl and Diemberger is subtly different from that given by Schmuck which, he says, is based on the conversation he had with Diemberger on the final ridge. There Diemberger had said that Buhl's painful foot had slowed him, but that he was still intent on reaching the top (as Schmuck says was also the essence of his conversation with Buhl near the Forepeak, and is, of course, exactly what Buhl did). Schmuck makes no mention of Diemberger having asked for permission to climb on alone, but perhaps the two men were saving their breath for climbing.

There is also disagreement about exactly what transpired when Diemberger reached the summit. Diemberger is still, after almost 50 years, upset by what he says happened there. He claims that Schmuck and Wintersteller hurried their departure from the top when they saw him approaching and that his request that they return with him to take a summit photograph

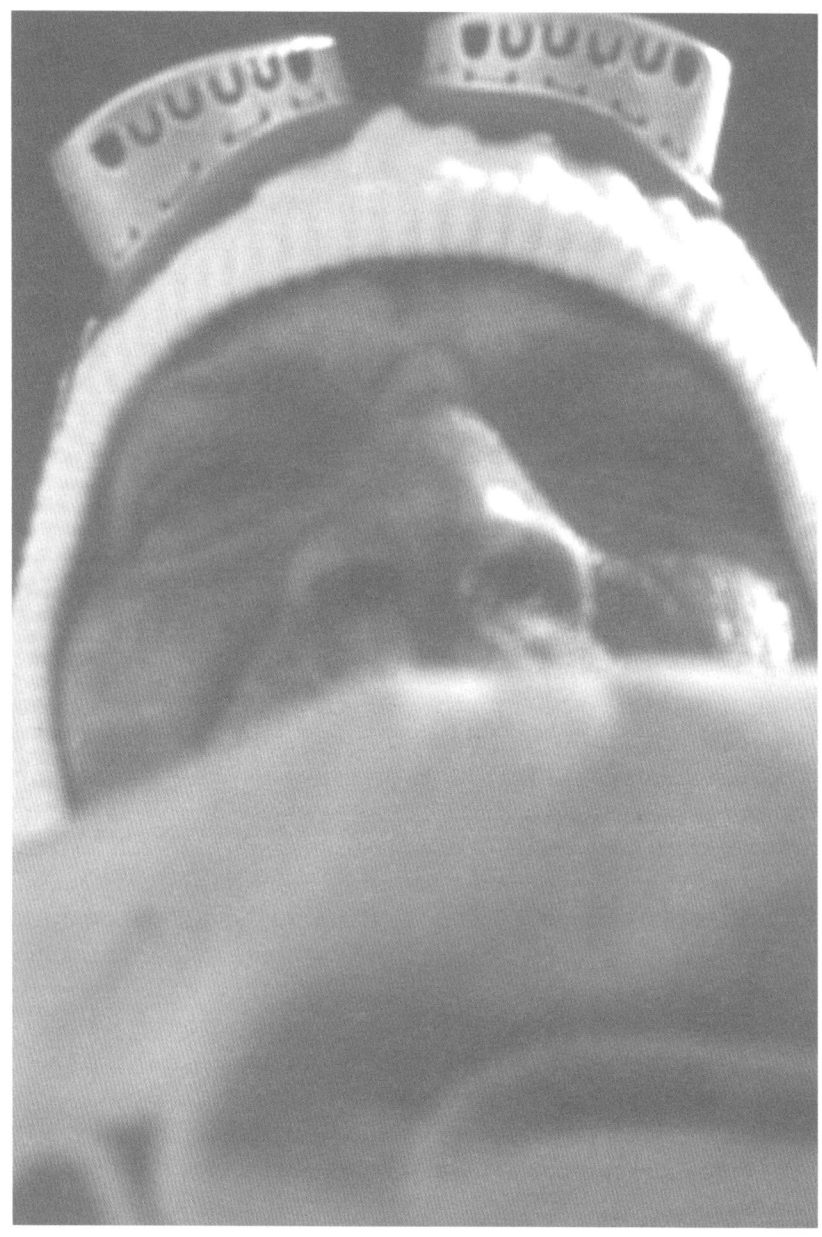

Wintersteller's attempt at a self-portrait on the summit.

was declined. Both Schmuck and Wintersteller claim this is nonsense. At first they were so overjoyed at summitting that they stood doing nothing much, just grateful not to have to go any further. Next they had taken photographs, a process (as Schmuck noted) that took a great deal of effort and concentration. Then they had hastily repacked their rucsacs and started down as they had already spent 45 minutes on the summit and there was a long way to go with night fast approaching. They claim to have been surprised to find Diemberger so close to the summit. He did not, they claim, ask for a photograph, but agree they would not have been keen to climb back to the summit to oblige him had he done so. A version of Diemberger's account of the meeting at the summit appeared in the first edition of Chris Bonington's book *Quest for Adventure*. Subsequent editions omitted the Broad Peak climb. In conversation with Diemberger he claimed that the omission was a result of Marcus Schmuck's lobbying of Bonington, something which Bonington denies, claiming that the omission was nothing more sinister than a need to reduce the page count.

Diemberger's account of the summit climb speaks of his sadness at leaving Buhl on the Forepeak ridge. At first, before asking Buhl's permission to continue on his own, Diemberger was not only sad but bitter that he (and Buhl) would not reach the top. When Buhl agreed to his continuing he was sad for the older man, leaving him sitting in the snow staring out at Nanga Parbat, 'his own mountain.' Diemberger pulled away from Buhl, following the long curving ridge towards the real summit. He claims that he actually ran along the ridge towards the summit and he must indeed have made up time to reach it just after Schmuck and Wintersteller had started down.

Diemberger, alone on the summit, picked out K2 (so obviously higher), Nanga Parbat, Mitre Peak and Masherbrum and peered down at the Baltoro. He recalled that it was Whit Sunday and that at home the fields and trees would be green. In order to get a better view of Tibet he climbed the cornice beyond the footprints of Schmuck and Wintersteller, finding it stable. Finally, with the light now fading, he turned to go, remembering that below him Buhl might still be waiting for him.

In fact Buhl had plodded on at a slower pace after Diemberger's departure. At some time around 6.15pm he met Wintersteller and, a little later, Schmuck. Both Buhl and Diemberger's accounts of Buhl's meeting with the two near the Forepeak have Buhl inquiring how long it will take him to reach the summit ('a good hour' is the reply), but Wintersteller, who was ahead of Schmuck, says that when he met Buhl and asked 'Are you going up?' Buhl did not respond verbally, only with a nod of the head. Wintersteller also says that Buhl had not only passed the Forepeak but the next rise on the ridge and that he would not have said an hour as it had only taken him 25 minutes from the summit to that point and the ridge from there was almost level: it seems that it actually took Buhl around 45 minutes to reach the top. Buhl continued along the ridge, passing the descending Schmuck and then meeting Diemberger as he was making his way down.

Diemberger's account of the meeting is poetic – coming towards him was the legend of the mountains, eyes fixed ahead, intent on reaching the summit despite the fact that night was closing fast. As Diemberger pointed out, Buhl had already spent one night out at 8000m, why not another? And so he turned to follow Buhl to the top. Buhl was now finding the going easier and at 7pm he and Diemberger reached the summit. There Diemberger took the photograph which has become iconic, Hermann Buhl with, behind him, Gasherbrum IV lit by the dying sun. In fact both Marcus Schmuck and Fritz Wintersteller say that this famous photograph seems to have been taken a short distance from the summit: there are rocks beyond Buhl and there were none at the summit, and the Gasherbrum ridge beyond does not exactly fit with the ridge line of a shot taken by Wintersteller from the summit. Schmuck's view is that the shot was probably taken 20m below the summit, some 50–100m horizontally from it.

The summit entry in Buhl's diary was matter-of-fact: 'At 7.00, just at sunset, we are at the top. I hurry before the sun has gone completely. I don't feel a thing at the moment, just wanting to take a few shots with the ice axe and the Bergland and Tirol pennants. I bind the Bergland pennant to the axe, putting the Tirol pennants into my pocket. When I go to take them out again I can't find them. They aren't in the snow either. I take two photos with the Bergland pennant and some panoramic shots. The light is great, everything in shadow, the sun only illuminating the spot where we are. It is setting, blood-red in colour.' However, in his typed report Buhl was far more lyrical: 'Chogolisa, Gasherbrum IV and K2 are illuminated by the dying light, and from one minute to the next the dark shadows ascend ever higher and extinguish the light on the surrounding peaks. But the highest ones are aflame, the whole horizon is a sea of red. Gasherbrum and Chogolisa are no longer white, they actually glow and finally they too are extinguished and only our peak is left flooded in sunlight. The snow becomes ever more red – now it is time to take the peak photos. We shake hands and say "Berg Heil!" I put my ice axe in the firn and take a few panoramic photos while there is still light. The sky becomes less intense, the moon is pale above us, and now the shadows climb towards us. It is 7.30 and while we follow the ridge to the pre-peak the light of the dying day still illuminates the snow. Only at the pre-peak does dusk really arrive, but then the moon lights the way down for us, when it is not hidden by the pre-peak or the steep rock ridge.'

Diemberger's account of the summit moments with Buhl is equally evocative: 'Straight ahead, against the last light, K2 reared its dark and massive head. Soft as velvet, all the colours merging into a single dark gleam. The snow suffused with a deep orange tint, while the sky was a remarkable azure. As I looked out, an enormous pyramid of darkness projected itself over the limitless wastes of Tibet, to lose itself in the haze of impalpable distance – the shadow of Broad Peak' (Diemberger, *Summits and Secrets*). At 7.30pm Diemberger noticed that when 'we looked down at the snow underfoot, to our amazement it seemed to be aglow.'

The two men left the summit and started back along the ridge in the last of the light. Below them Wintersteller was forging ahead of Schmuck. By 8pm, less than two hours after meeting Buhl, he arrived at Camp 3. The time of his arrival was all he set down in his diary, other than the fact that he reached the camp so quickly 'by sliding down the greater part of the way on my behind.' Schmuck's account was more expansive: 'Fritz is already ahead on the descent, while I put little specimens of the various rocks from the summit ridge into my anorak. Shortly before reaching the pre-peak on my descent, I meet Hermann on his way up. Despite being in a bad way he has pulled himself together and begins the ascent to the main peak although it is already dangerously late. We couldn't have held him back, because the goal was that all of us would stand at Broad Peak's summit. A further attempt would have taken weeks and each incursion into this zone requires a lot of time to recover – once already we have been taught this lesson, and I wouldn't like to guarantee that our health would sustain a further attempt. In both directions there is the greatest hurry. I often sit in the snow in order to give my faculties a chance to recover. Below, in the Wind Gap, Fritz is already in the last of the sunlight and lengthens the rope in order to make the descent easier. At 7pm I reach the Wind Gap. Because I am in a hurry I cling to the rope and slide down on it as quickly as possible.

'I have to stop several times in order to catch my breath. I see Fritz 200m further down sitting in a hollow. He is by the rucsac [which the pair had left on their ascent]. Is there still a little tea left? – that thought occupies me at the moment. My mouth and throat are terribly dry. Carefully I make my way down the ice hump below the Wind Gap, then I am standing on the steep snow flank. Sitting on my bottom I slide down into the hollow, using my ice axe as a brake. The rucsac, the Thermos, the sip of tea and then innumerable breaths. With this limited rest I recover a little. On the glacier 2500m below the shadows of night have long since set in. The snow on the peaks still gleams white, while the moon shines down over Broad Peak's ridge. A moonlit night – we are lucky. I keep to Fritz's tracks, innumerable times I fall backwards to recover from the exhausting descent. Lying on my back, looking up at the stars I am content. Then I move a little closer to Camp 3, the two tents distinctly visible at the ice knee. It is very quiet around the camp. I throw my ski pole and ice axe behind our tent, take off my crampons, over-trousers and anorak in front of the tent then plunge through the opening. Fritz is already deep in sleep. I follow his example immediately. Lying in my snowed-over sleeping bag I am pleased with our good fortune. Worried about our fellow-climbers who are still descending, but overwhelmed by tired-ness I end this Whit Sunday, one so significant for all of us, at about 9pm.'

Far above, the moon which assisted Schmuck was a lifeline for Buhl and Diemberger. It was dark by the time they reached the Forepeak, moonlight allowing them to pick their way slow-ly, but safely, down to the Wind Gap. Buhl wrote that occasion-ally the pair belayed each other during that descent, the first time there is any indication that either had carried a rope. The fixed rope from the Wind Gap allowed them to reach the snow. At this point the account in Diemberger's book ends, though the climb down the steep snow slope by moonlight while exhaust-ed must have been a trial, the survival of the two men a tribute to their determination. Buhl was a little, but not much, more forthcoming: 'Desperately the eye seeks out the boulders and the tents, which must be near now. Our feet are heavy and our ankles are in pain from working the steep, hard ice. Finally, the first boulder and the outlines of the two tents. It is past midnight before we crawl into the tents and close them behind us. We have nothing to eat or drink, wanting only to rest and immedi-ately get into our sleeping bags. As before a deathly sleep descends upon us and it is not until late the next morning that we wake.'

Wintersteller, as always the realist, noted 'Marcus arrives at 8.30pm, Hermann and Kurt one and a half hours after midnight. They spent five hours longer in the "death zone" than us.'

In conversation with Diemberger he raises the fact that Schmuck and Wintersteller were in their sleeping bags and probably asleep before he and Buhl returned. He says it would have been good had they waited to make sure their colleagues were safe. But there was little Schmuck and Wintersteller could have done. The team had run out of fuel the night before so there was no hope of making the late arrivals any tea or warm food. There was also no liquid at the camp as the 5 litres they had been able to make the previous evening had been consumed during the day. There was also little chance of Schmuck and Wintersteller mounting a rescue attempt that night exhausted as they were. They were also cold so sitting outside the tents waiting was not an option. Diemberger admits all this, but nevertheless still feels that there was a lack of comradeship in the other pair's behaviour.

On Whit Monday, 10 June, Schmuck and Wintersteller were up by 9am. The weather was poor, the wind getting up. Hastily they packed their tent and equipment ready for the descent to Camp 2. Wintersteller made no mention of the other two members of the team in his account, while Schmuck noted only that 'Hermann and Kurt stay put as usual', a remark born of the frustration of making trail so frequently, but one which seems a lit-

The telegram to the Edelweiss Club in Austria announcing the successful climb. The text reads 'Hurrah, 9 June all 4 Broad Peak'.

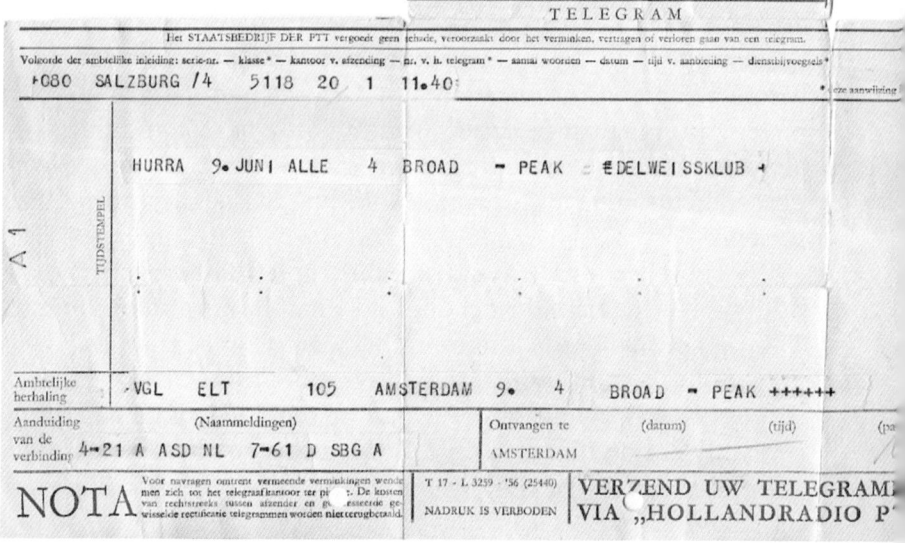

tle unkind given the epic day the others had just endured. At 9.30am the early risers left Camp 3 for the last time, carrying all their equipment. Their progress with huge rucsacs was slow. At the Herrligkoffer depot they collected a 40m rope, then continued to Camp 2, reaching it at about 11.30am where 'after a cigarette I enjoy the hot tea that Marcus has prepared and eat ox-tongue salad, followed by a rather long nap' (Wintersteller). The rest revived the two of them and they decided to try to make Base Camp that day. They packed up most of the camp, leaving only enough for the others. A kitbag was stuffed with three tents, two airbeds, a kitchen set and two sleeping bags. The plan was to lower this with the 40m rope. Wintersteller headed off downhill, but went too far, so that when Schmuck lowered the kitbag it stopped above him. Schmuck let go the rope, but 'instead of sliding, [the kitbag] begins to bump, and I can only grab hold of it with a supreme effort' (Wintersteller) – 'I let go of the kitbag and its rope. It's a while before I see the kitbag sliding past Fritz at full throttle. Fritz runs after the rope and manages to stop it. Quite an achievement at 6200m!' (Schmuck).

They struggled to haul the heavy bag to Camp 1, but below that the descent was easier as they could lower the bag directly down the slope. At the narrow gully Schmuck came up with a novel idea: 'I sit on the kitbag and slide down to the glacier.' Leaving the bag at the glacier they crossed, calling out to Qader at Base Camp. 'At 7.15pm Qader greets us, beaming with joy' (Wintersteller) – 'Qader comes towards us, he is pleased. We shake hands and are glad to be back down here. We talk a lot. Qader cooks. Then we toast Broad Peak and Qader's 25th birthday' (Schmuck).

6
Skil Brum and Chogolisa

During the night at Base Camp Wintersteller's face and neck started to itch terribly. From his youth he has had a sunlight allergy which causes him to break out in a rash and the strong sun at altitude during the summit climb had caused a recurrence. At daybreak he searched out a French skin cream with which he treated the condition. He and Schmuck then wrote postcards while Qader fussed over them. At the same time Schmuck was watching the slopes of the mountain for some sign of the others. At around 11.30am he saw them descending separately towards Camp 1 and assumed that they had spent the night in Camp 2. He thought that the pair should arrive by 2pm, but they did not. By 6pm he and Wintersteller were very worried, but then at 7pm they saw the two slowly approaching, absolutely exhausted.

Buhl's diary account of the descent started with an acknowledgement of a conversation Schmuck also records: 'Markus thinks we should take our tent down with us too, and just throw away the ski poles, thermos and pots. We want to leave at midday. We have no fuel left and can't cook anything. We take down the tent, but our rucksacks are already so heavy that it's not possible to take any more with us and on top of this everything including provisions, gas canisters etc. are still up here, so we stow it away and decide to come back up for it. We leave Camp III at 1pm. It is a difficult and strenuous descent despite the ropes and I long to be on the plateau. I am in Camp II at 5pm. Kurt had rushed ahead, reaching it an hour earlier and had

Skil Brum, to the right, from high on Broad Peak.

151

made something warm to drink. Markus and Fritz had already left again without leaving us anything to drink and have taken the gas connection with them. Not much fuel here anymore, so soon couldn't do any more cooking. We went to sleep tired and hungry.' In this account Buhl concedes that he and Diemberger leave equipment behind having decided to come back for it. The removal of the gas connector from Camp 2 was unfortunate, but Buhl's report suggests the pair found enough fuel for their Primus to make hot drinks.

The next day the descent continued: 'It's only with difficulty that we get out of our sleeping bags. Cold melted snow and biscuit for breakfast. At midday we descend to Camp I. My rucsac is terribly heavy and the snow bad (a slippery layer on ice). My crampons hold, but I slip several times and can only hold on with difficulty. 2pm in Camp I. I make tea but there is no sugar and without sugar it tastes bad. We wait for the midday heat to subside then, at 4pm we descend, cautiously, because it is getting ever more dangerous with ice under the snow. The sleeping bags stay at Camp I. At the Godwin-Austen Glacier we have difficulty finding our way through the many pools and glacial lakes but at 7pm we are in Base Camp. Kadar recognises us and comes towards us with a cry of joy. Fritz and Markus sit apathetically in the kitchen. They say they had spotted us and had been worried that we took so long. They had considered whether to set out towards us. Then Kadar told me that Markus had told him that it's not easy to be the leader of an expedition when one has responsibility for others. There wasn't much available to eat, but Kadar immediately warmed up two tins of food. We were almost out of our wits with hunger.'

Buhl's final expedition report ended with an amplification of the final moments to Base Camp and a recognition that the team had achieved something remarkable: 'The evening grants us great views and I stop more than once to take it all in, the last light on Chogolisa, while Kurt stumbles on ahead of me, complaining about the many ponds and the soft snow. "What are you moaning about, Kurt," I ask him, "This is part of the mountain too, and if it was right for us to reach the summit we should put up with this as well", although I too had to repress some choice words … Broad Peak has been conquered, by the shortest, most favourable route, without using porters on the mountain, by all four team members – what more could we want? We can be content, and that we certainly are. In order to make our happiness complete, the mailrunners come within a few days and bring everyone something from home, all of it pleasant and each of us goes back to his tent and buries his bearded face in a letter.'

Over a meal Buhl complained of mild frostbite and he and Diemberger admitted that they had left almost all their gear on the mountain, some at Camp 3 and more at Camp 2. By the next day Buhl and Diemberger had recovered enough to dismiss the fact that they would have to climb back up to clear the top camps: '"As soon as the weather picks up, we'll get the stuff, that'll be peanuts for us". Well that's fine by us, and we will clear out Camp 1' (Wintersteller). Diemberger gave both Buhl and Schmuck precautionary anti-frostbite injections (with Wintersteller noting that 'Kurt does this very conscientiously. I wouldn't have thought it of him').

Buhl's implicit suggestion of team contentment didn't last. On the day after his arrival back at Base Camp he wrote 'Can breathe through lips and nose again. Very tense atmosphere. Kurt asks Fritz about ointment, at which Fritz yells at him loudly. I try to come between them and it is only then that Fritz calms down. Markus is intent on having his own ointment for the frostbite on his feet, and demands this although he knows there isn't much left for the next fourteen days. And he isn't much bothered about me, although my feet are in a much worse state.'

There was worse to come, Buhl and Diemberger being asked to sign postcards which Schmuck and Wintersteller had written. Schmuck noted that 'obviously they don't like the contents but you can't argue with the truth.' A significant entry. That evening Schmuck wrote that 'K2, rising above a sea of mist, glows surreally in the moonlight. How we long to be up there, but our health is more important.'

The weather now turned unpleasant, causing Schmuck to rejoice that they had had the best day of the month for their summit climb. Wintersteller wrote to the Austrian Embassy in Karachi asking officials there to send on the 700 postcards they had written: '300 Hermann, 200 Marcus, 108 Fritz, 70 Kurt. The postcards show the western peak of Broad Peak, from a 1909 photo by the great Vittorio Sella.' The letter went with the mail-runners who had arrived with letters from home. The remainder of the day was spent resting, reading and re-reading the newly delivered letters.

Having avoided a diary comment on the postcards on 12 June when Schmuck mentions the tension they create, Buhl's entire entry for 13 June dealt with the issue: 'Major writing day. No one has time to cook. Marcus writing inflammatory postcards to the whole of Salzburg. He would almost save himself money if he commissioned a mail drop to every household in town. He is determined to let the whole world know that his was the first rope to the summit at 1505 [sic]. Fritz's cards are no less con-frontational. Both of them are writing almost exclusively to personal friends. In the evening I remind them of such things as solidarity and common achievement, and how we had always agreed that all four of us should make the summit. I pressed on them that we had achieved something unique which it would be a shame to diminish with these pettinesses. We would be seriously diminishing ourselves. I made myself very clear.'

Schmuck and Wintersteller both say that Buhl argued that there should be no mention of the fact that the four reached the summit at different times and was content only when they all agreed, though in his diary Schmuck noted that Buhl's ambition regarding Broad Peak had finally come to light, adding sarcastically that it was a pity that he had not shown the same ambition at 7500m. From the diaries it does seem that now, relaxed at Base Camp, Buhl had a different view about reaching the top to the one he had displayed during the summit climb.

There are also curious entries about Diemberger's behaviour. In his diary Schmuck noted that during conversations 'Kurt interrupts with cheeky comments', but added that 'everyone calms down again.' Wintersteller was more blunt: 'Since Hermann has stopped calling him to order, Kurt becomes ever more insolent, threatens violence, mumbles something about judo throws, and gets more and more unbearable.' It would seem that with his own, understandable, ambitions of being first to the summit having been thwarted, Diemberger was upset and, presumably, annoyed that Schmuck and Wintersteller were reluctant to agree that no mention should be made of the different summit times.

The entries about the discussion on reaching the summit are interesting. Both Schmuck and Wintersteller claim that they kept to the agreement not to say that the four reached the top at different times and that only after Diemberger stated in his own book that this was not the case did they change their stories. Yet Schmuck's book, published in 1958, states quite clearly that he and Wintersteller were first to the summit, that Diemberger was next and Buhl last.

Buhl's writing the next day (14 June) was again mostly taken up with the reporting of the climb and the need to avoid spelling out the timing of the summit climbs, and with the relationship of the two teams: 'Fritz has changed his tune, he tries to get on the right side of Kurt and myself. Markus is difficult. He wants to send telegrams which do not include the words "the whole team". But we are against this and Kurt determinedly pushes this point. We demand a copy of the letter to Geoghan (the Austrian Consul in Karachi) with the actual text of the telegrams he has been asked to send. Markus is making deals with the Captain (Qader Saeed) behind my back about the end date for the expedition. Without consulting us he wants to order porters for the end of June just because he has to leave earlier. He shows no interest in staying on any longer. I, however, have quite a few things left on my agenda. Advertising shots, taking down the camp, excursions, etc. I remind him that as leader with respect to climbing I too have a say in the matter, and he doesn't like it. I tell him that the equipment won't be taken away until everything has been dealt with. It's such dictatorial behaviour to make such an important decision without asking anyone. After much to-ing and fro-ing we decide upon 5 July, but Markus wants yet another compromise after this. Earlier we were to stay three months but now it is just six weeks. However it remains the 5 July.'

Schmuck resting on Skil Brum during the successful ascent. Beyond him is Broad Peak.

Clearly the expedition is now falling apart. Buhl's references in this entry to 'we' and 'us' seems to mean Diemberger and himself: even more than on Broad Peak there are now two distinct teams operating. Wintersteller denies any suggestion that we was trying to 'get on the right side' of Buhl, merely that he was trying to smooth things over as the constant bickering was getting on his nerves. The discussion on the timing of the withdrawal is also interesting. Schmuck's diary, right from the start, implies an end of June withdrawal, but Diemberger says that Buhl always had a longer trip planned and had spoken about the possibility of major climbs after Broad Peak (including a traverse of K2). It would seem that the two of them (Buhl and Schmuck) had arrived with different objectives and timescales in mind.

Fed up with the bickering, Wintersteller spent most of the day in Qader's tent talking with him. It was the start of a friendship which has lasted until the present day (Qader also remains very friendly with Schmuck: the three men have visited each other's homes and still keep in touch). As a result of this blossoming relationship, when Wintersteller and Schmuck went up to clear Camp 1 on 16 June they took Qader with them, giving him his first experience on crampons. Despite being troubled by altitude Qader reached the camp. The two Austrians packed the camp into a kitbag – during the packing five eagles glided past just 100m away – and slid it back down to the glacier, reaching Base Camp again at 3pm after a nine hour day. Qader was delighted with the trip. Less ecstatic were Buhl and Diemberger who had stayed at Base Camp all day and were, Schmuck says, 'lukewarm.' He continues: 'We sleep for a few hours until Hermann wakes us for dinner. Afterwards I can't go back to sleep despite my tiredness because I am thinking about a book that we could write.' The events of the next weeks destroy the concept of the book Schmuck was considering. Instead he wrote one on his own. *Broad Peak 8047m: Meine Bergfahrten mit Hermann Buhl* was published in 1958. It has never been translated into English.

On 17 June Buhl and Diemberger left for Camp 3. The expedition had now, it seems, finally divided into two as Schmuck and Wintersteller, who followed them as far as the equipment dump at the base of the west face, were obviously intent on attempting another peak without waiting for their team mates to return.

Buhl and Diemberger left at 5.45am, Schmuck and Wintersteller at 7am. Wintersteller noted that: 'It's a wonderful morning, we take a lot of pictures of the glacial lakes and the surrounding peaks. When we arrive at the place where we had deposited the kitbag, we can still see our companions. They haven't made that much progress – so much for "peanuts"!' The last part of the entry is a caustic reference to the earlier Buhl/Diemberger claim of how easy it would be for them to clear the top camp. Schmuck and Wintersteller divided up the contents of the kitbag left at the peak's base the previous day and returned to Base Camp.

Buhl and Diemberger climbed up to Camp 2 which they found completely snowed in. Next day (18 June) 'Kurt goes up to Camp III to fetch the tent and camp equipment while I take down the ropes ready for removal, and cook at Camp II until Kurt arrives. Massive amount of fresh snow. Cooker isn't working properly. In the evening I ate too much concentrated soup – didn't sleep, bad diarrhoea.' Next day Buhl's mood deteriorates: 'Up at 8am, terribly cold. I curse Fritz and the camp, which was his idea. The sun doesn't reach the camp for 5 hours, while in front and on the plateau it is already shining. There it is warm. Average temperature -20°C, without gloves you can barely do any work. First we go to plateau to get warm. My feet are ice-cold. Begin moving at about 10am. There's still a lot in Camp II, provisions for fourteen days with a lot of equipment: each of us has a rucsac and a kit bag with two tents and about 60kg of equipment. Moving things in the heat is a great strain and the bag won't slide. 4pm at Camp II [sic: Buhl must mean Camp 1]. Kurt, after I tell him off because he never listens, throws a tantrum, and has a real go at me. 6.30pm at the glacier. Bag and rope stay behind, I take only my personal equipment. Kurt breaks through the ice into a glacier stream, up to half of him in the icy water. 8pm at camp. Kadar is alone and explains that Fritz and Markus went to the Savoia Glacier for 3–4 days the day before yesterday. Although they had told us they would clear the camps, they had only taken the tents. They had taken nothing else down with them. Went straight to bed. Slept well.'

The clearing of the camps is still, half a century later, a contentious issue. Schmuck and Wintersteller are adamant they had taken their half of the equipment from both Camps 3 and 2, and had cleared Camp 1. When Buhl and Diemberger returned to Base Camp after their clearance day Buhl noted in his diary that 'Kader has already told him (Wintersteller) that it was wrong to leave us to clear the camp, while they went off on an expedition without our knowledge to a mountain we had always discussed climbing together.' This quote was used in the Höfler/Messner biography of Buhl and not only incensed Wintersteller but also Qader Saeed. In conversation, and later in writing, Qader said that this statement was not true. He went on to say that as Buhl could barely make himself understood in English he could not have had any conversation of that form with him. Qader says that he suspects that Buhl was misinformed of his opinion by Diemberger who did most of the talking for the pair because his English was much better. Qader says that in his view Diemberger often had an ulterior motive when talking with him (Qader). It would be easy to question these opinions on the grounds that they were offered years later and might be influenced by events which have occurred since the expedition, but Schmuck's diary for 17 June (that is, prior to the Skil Brum climb) noted that 'Qader intends to report Kurt to the governor!' The governor in question was local Political Resident/governor Lt Col Yusuf, who was Qader's superior officer. As well as becoming increasingly exasperated with Diemberger's habit of using his English to demand special favours as though they were team requests, Qader did not like what he saw as Diemberger's lack of comradeship which, he considered, exemplified a consistent, selfish attitude. Qader therefore intended to tell the authorities that Diemberger should never again be allowed into Pakistan. He says that he did this, though in a subtle way as he did not wish to emphasise divisions in the expedition, particularly after Buhl's death. But as far as he was concerned, the decision to ban Diemberger had been agreed. Qader was therefore astonished when during a conversation I told him that Diemberger had returned to the Karakoram in 1984 and 1986. He could only assume that the passage of time had caused the original decision to be forgotten.

Fritz Wintersteller at the summit of Skil Brum. The cairn of stones he built can be seen behind him. The summit was sharp and the snow conditions poor so that Schmuck and Wintersteller could not stand together.

As further evidence that he was not opposed to the Schmuck/Wintersteller venture Qader says that at his request weather forecasts for the expedition were announced over the radio and he would pass this information on to the team. Around 15/16 June Qader had heard that there was to be a period of settled weather which the team should take advantage of. He also says that he was enthusiastic that Skil Brum should be climbed (Wintersteller noted that 'Qader agrees with our plan' as confirmation of this). It was, at that time, an unnamed peak and in an unexplored area and so its ascent would be, in part, an exploration of Pakistani territory. Qader therefore knew the ascent would have his superiors' approval. Schmuck and Wintersteller still feel that given the weather window and the certainty that Buhl and Diemberger would be away for at least two days they were justified in going to Skil Brum. They also say that Skil Brum had never been mentioned as a potential team target (it is certainly not mentioned in any of the diaries), and that Buhl and Diemberger were not just clearing the top camps, but retrieving their personal equipment which they had left on the hill: without that equipment they could not attempt any further climbs.

What is clear is that there was annoyance (at least) on the part of Buhl and Diemberger that the other two had gone off alone and been very successful and it is a matter of debate what effect the decision had on subsequent events. For Buhl Skil Brum was the last straw: 'Now my patience is really at an end, I must play my cards close to my chest.'

Skil Brum

The Skil Brum climb began on 18 June, Schmuck and Wintersteller leaving Base Camp at 4am, crossing the Godwin-Austen Glacier and turning left to follow the Savoia Glacier. At the point where the Praqpa Glacier meets the Savoia, they put on skis and followed the Praqpa. After a rest to escape the strong midday sun they climbed to the col at the head of the glacier. The col lies between two 7000m peaks: they decided to attempt the one on the right and climbed up to about 6000m where they found a camp site well sheltered from both avalanches and the wind. They were in their sleeping bags by 5pm, cooking from them until 6pm when they tried to sleep.

The following day the two men started early. It was a beautiful day, but very cold. They climbed steep (40°–50°) slopes, sometimes on ice, sometimes on soft snow which threatened to avalanche. For once Wintersteller was having a bad day and Schmuck did most of the trail breaking. At 4pm they reached a pointed summit which Wintersteller's altimeter measured at 7420m: the peak was later surveyed at 7360m. The summit was so sharp that the two men did not dare to actually stand on it, fearing it would collapse, and only one at a time could get close to it. From the top, where Wintersteller erected a stone cairn, there was a fantastic view of Broad Peak, which looked very steep, and of Paiju Peak and the Mustagh Tower. They had climbed the highest peak of the Savoia. At that time the peak was unnamed: Schmuck and Wintersteller wanted to name it after G.O. Dyhrenfurth, but it was named Skil Brum by the Pakistani Government. On the descent Schmuck was overwhelmed by an attack of high-altitude cough, coughing so hard he was sick into the snow. But even that could not extinguish the sheer joy of the ascent, a joy which shines through his account of the day: 'Slogging down in deep snow, then frozen snow and an ice channel. A great strain. I jump over a crevasse then ski down to the tent – marvellous! 19.30 at the tent, cooking in candlelight. The cooker falls over, but we aren't bothered, just pleased and happy at our success. About 9pm to bed! Very cold!'

The joy extended into the next day, when, after a breakfast of juice and Ovaltine, 'we descend with unusual speed and much less effort over the frozen snow between the crevasses. We stop several times in order to calm our breathing, we are skiing at 6000m after all! And with 15kg on our backs. I have a fall and as a result the Thermos is destroyed. We deliberately swing down in beautiful curves to the Savoia Glacier, and after a short rest we continue schussing down on our short skis. I would have loved to call out in joy but during the descent I didn't have enough air. At the beginning of the system of crevasses we leave a tent, air-beds, food, fuel and cooker so we won't have to carry

Gasherbrum II, Gasherbrum IV and Chogolisa from Skil Brum.

it from Base Camp on a future visit, then continue descending. At one point we have to carry our skis across a crevasse, but otherwise we wangle our way right back to Base Camp which we reach at 8.30am' (Schmuck).

At the camp only Diemberger was up: he and Buhl had only returned the previous evening at 8pm. Schmuck writes that 'instead of being happy for us we got only an envious lack of response from him [Diemberger]. This doesn't surprise us!' The attitude might well not have come as a surprise, but given the circumstances it was optimistic of Schmuck to expect anything different. Wintersteller also noted that the second pair were not happy with their success in a letter to a friend written at Base Camp while the others were on Chogolisa: 'is it so difficult for one mountaineer to feel joy at the success of another?' In the

Hermann Buhl's note left in the Base Camp kitchen before his departure for Chogolisa.

same letter Wintersteller gave his view of why the other pair had been slow in reaching Broad Peak's summit. Buhl, he said, had not been in good shape throughout the expedition: Diemberger lacked experience. He then made an interesting, if controversial, point, that Diemberger was like some German climbers, great at the hard climbing, mediocre at the mundane stuff: Diemberger was a good climber on difficult ice, but not experienced and so not good at the daily grind of mountaineering. After this charitable assessment he noted that Diemberger was also 'a pain in the ass.'

Diemberger spent the afternoon of 20 June – the day Schmuck and Wintersteller returned from Skil Brum – packing his rucsac. When asked where he was going Wintersteller wrote that Diemberger said he 'intends to go to the area of the Gasherbrums for 5–7 days, in order to take pictures and to investigate the area's potential for a future expedition.' Schmuck was more specific in his diary, saying that Diemberger 'potters around all day in order to ready himself for his wilful attempt at Gasherbrum IV.' He noted that Diemberger had neither his permission, as expedition leader, nor that of Qader for this venture. But, joining the conversation, Buhl said that he would take full responsibility. On hearing this from me Qader Saeed was angry, pointing out that Buhl had no right to assume responsibility for any venture which did not have the express permission of the Pakistan government or himself. But more of that later.

Buhl's statement must have placed Schmuck in a difficult situation. The verbal agreement with Buhl relating to decisions on the mountain could be called into play, and short of tying Diemberger down it is hard to see exactly what Schmuck could have done if the younger man was adamant about leaving. Wintersteller obviously felt for Schmuck, noting that 'Hermann says that he takes full responsibility. We just have to accept that.' Carrying a vast rucsac – which Schmuck estimated at 33kg – Diemberger set off at 4.30pm. It was a strange time to choose as the snow, soft in the afternoon sun, would make walking hard work. Diemberger returned at 5.15pm. Schmuck wondered 'why doesn't he leave early in the morning? He prefers walking

A photograph taken during Wintersteller's abortive attempt to reach the Skyang La while Buhl and Diemberger were on Chogolisa.

in the soft snow – as wilful as ever.' Sure enough, Diemberger departed again later.

Next day when Schmuck got up for breakfast he found a note from Buhl in the meal tent: 'Dear Marcus! Because I didn't want to leave Kurt alone, I followed after him early this morning. I'll return with Kurt in 5–7 days' time. In the meantime you could continue our work in the Savoia Glacier area. All the best and good luck.' In his diary Schmuck wondered where they had gone, adding 'only the gods know!' before a final note 'Quiet in the camp – marvellous.' Wintersteller also reported the note, his final entry regretting that 'Hermann and Kurt didn't bring their things down straight away as we did. It would have saved them another climb to Camp 3 when, like us, they could have been attempting a 7000m peak instead.'

Buhl's departure, and subsequent death on Chogolisa, is one of the significant moments in mountaineering history, and has to an extent overshadowed the brilliance of the Austrians' achievement on Broad Peak. It is therefore worth considering what lay behind it. Wintersteller claims that on the evening before his departure Buhl told Schmuck that he was still feeling very weak, though Schmuck can no longer confirm this (shrugging and saying 'perhaps'). Buhl's comment may have been a ploy, said to disarm the others, as Diemberger claims that the decision to leave separately was always part of their plan. But it was worth recalling that in his diary entry for 18 June Buhl had noted his 'bad diarrhoea'. The extract from Buhl's diary found by the Japanese on Chogolisa, quoted by Diemberger and, subsequently, by Höfler/Messner in their books, suggests Buhl was in good shape on his last climb, and this has been the story told by Diemberger in several of his books. But Diemberger has not always told that story, one writer quoting him as saying that when the pair turned back on Chogolisa Buhl was unusually tired.

Qader's role is also interesting. He admits now that he knew Buhl and Diemberger were going to Chogolisa, though he had told them that the weather forecast was poor. He denies a suggestion of Diemberger's that he actually agreed to go with the pair to Chogolisa, only to change his mind later. Qader also claims that at one point he told Buhl he should wait for Schmuck's return, as he was leader of the expedition, to discuss the climb with him. That was a suggestion Buhl was unlikely to have viewed with any enthusiasm. In conversation with Qader he said that Schmuck and Wintersteller had arrived back after Buhl and Diemberger had departed. He was adamant on this point and was clearly taken aback when the Schmuck and Wintersteller diaries proved otherwise. Qader's view was that Schmuck and Wintersteller's arrival after Buhl and Diemberger's departure explained why he had not told them where the latter pair had gone, though that can only be partially true as he maintained his silence on the matter throughout the time until Diemberger's return.

It is not difficult to understand why Buhl and Diemberger would have wanted to climb Chogolisa. Already annoyed, rightly or wrongly, by the summit climb on Broad Peak and the subsequent wording of the team postcards, then aggrieved at having to clear the top camps, they would have realised that a lightning Alpine ascent of Chogolisa would have readjusted the balance between the two pairs, particularly after the ascent of Skil Brum. Even if he was still weak, Buhl's competitiveness and self-belief can easily be seen to have been the deciding factors. For Diemberger it was a chance to accompany the great man on what might have been another ground-breaking ascent. That neither man told the other two Austrians of their plan is consistent with the idea that this was, in part, a payback for perceived injustices. After the three surviving members of the expedition returned, Diemberger was questioned about Chogolisa by the Alpenverein. He admitted that he and Buhl had been upset by the Skil Brum climb. It was, he said, a *schweinerei*, an absolute outrage. Diemberger also said that the leadership issue had been a factor. Buhl was annoyed that his orders and opinions as climbing leader had been ignored on Broad Peak, and that he had not even been consulted about Skil Brum. Buhl was torn between wanting to go home because tensions in the team were now so bad and wanting to do more climbing. Chogolisa had the advantage of allowing pride to be restored and, said Diemberger, of being in the opposite direction to the Savoia where Buhl thought Schmuck would go again.

Qader's position was more delicate. It is not possible to know what pressure he felt he was under when being told about the Chogolisa climb. Qader says that Buhl came to his tent at one point and gave him a number of films. Qader says he did not need these, but the fact that he raised the issue at all suggests he (Qader) was suspicious of the motive behind the gesture. Qader says that this incident was after Diemberger's departure and that he had told Buhl he should bring Diemberger back as soon as possible and that an attempt on Chogolisa was illegal. But by Qader's own admission Buhl's English was not up to such a conversation and Buhl left very early in the morning before anyone was up. Much more likely is that the incident took place before Diemberger departed and probably before Schmuck and Wintersteller returned from Skil Brum.

By not telling Schmuck what he knew – and it is clear he did not – Qader seems to have been avoiding what might have been a confrontation with the expedition leader. An illegal ascent of Chogolisa was likely to be viewed quite differently from the Skil Brum climb by the authorities. Skil Brum was unnamed, the Savoia range unexplored. Chogolisa was a known and significant mountain. Its ascent would have caused problems, both for the Austrians and Qader. Possibly Qader hoped the Buhl/Diemberger attempt would be curtailed by the predicted bad weather letting him off the hook. Certainly after Buhl's death Qader did not admit to having agreed to the climb, probably a very wise course.

During the period from Buhl's departure on 21 June to Diemberger's return a week later Schmuck and Wintersteller did very little. Their planned climb of a nearby 6000m peak was aborted because of the bad weather that Qader had warned Buhl and Diemberger about was imminent, and Wintersteller's planned excursion to Windy Gap (Skyang La), the famous col to the north-east of K2, also failed. Wintersteller wanted to look over the col into Sinkiang and took the now-enthusiastic Qader. Unfortunately the pair fell into a small crevasse, Wintersteller bashing his left leg so badly that the shinbone was exposed. In pain and limping he and Qader slowly returned to Base Camp, the little expedition ending in farce when they took an 'involuntary bath in a freezing moraine stream.'

On the 24th and 25th Wintersteller noted in his diary what foul weather Buhl and Diemberger were having and what a shame it was for them as they were primarily on a photography trip (as he thought). The two mailrunners arrived and Wintersteller noted his admiration for them – '... really tough guys. The route is very dangerous and difficult, especially in bad weather.' He also complained about his shin, the leg now swollen and so painful it was preventing him from sleeping and also from helping with the packing of the expedition's aluminium chests, a necessary chore as the porters would soon be arriving for the return trip.

Schmuck's diary for this same period was also filled with the minutiae of camp life – birdsong was heard for the first time, a rabbit (?) ate the porridge. The absentees had turned the camp into – 'Pure bliss. Hermann and Kurt are away and there is quiet, order and peace.' But he, too, was worried about the pair: not only was the weather bad but the radio was now telling them that the monsoon was fast approaching Nanda Devi. Schmuck was also very worried about what exactly Buhl and Diemberger were doing. Had their photography trip turned into a more serious undertaking? If it had, and 'they try to climb Hidden Peak, a thought that I wouldn't put past them although physically they aren't up to it, then they would be detained by the Pakistani authorities. Do we really need this?' The arrival of the mailrunners took the edge off his concerns as he read and re-read the letters from his wife, but the next day the worry returned: 'It is the eighth day since they left and Hermann wanted to be back after 5–7 days, and Kurt after 8–10 days. They are therefore still on schedule, but nevertheless we scan the moraine to see if anyone is coming.'

At 4.40pm one of the mailrunners shouted that a Sahib was coming. Schmuck later wrote: 'I look out of the little tent window and see Kurt approaching, half collapsed. I quickly, fearfully say "Something has happened" and in the same moment Fritz and I are outside. We hurry the few metres towards him and ask "What the hell is going on?" "Hermann has fallen on Chogolisa at 7300m", the exhausted Kurt replies sobbing. We are shocked. We immediately take a detailed report from which we learn the tragic events that led to the fall.' Wintersteller wrote: 'We rush out of the tent and see Kurt arriving alone. "Hermann fell on Chogolisa". Marcus calls back "That can't be true!" I curse. Qader lets out a shrill cry and goes back into the tent to be alone.'

As soon as the initial shock had passed the three Austrians set down a statement dealing with the events leading to Buhl's death. It was written by Wintersteller, in the presence of Schmuck, from Diemberger's description. Each man then signed the statement.

Chogolisa. This shot was taken from the Broad Peak Base Camp.

Chogolisa

The statement tells the story of the attempt on Chogolisa which Diemberger later recounted in the first of his books published in English, a story which has been retold in many places since. Diemberger left Base Camp on the evening of 20 June, Buhl following him the next day and catching him later that same day at the site of the 1934 IHE's Camp IV. On 22 June the pair started towards the Kaberi Pass which lies to the east of Chogolisa's main summit. The next day the weather was bad – Buhl and Diemberger were experiencing the same poor weather that kept Schmuck and Wintersteller in Base Camp. On 24 June they climbed to the Kaberi Pass. Diemberger quotes an entry from Buhl's last diary (a quote which has been used many times subsequently: the diary was retrieved in 1958 from the Austrian camp by the Japanese climbers Fujihara and Hirai who were following the same route during the first ascent of Chogolisa) which stated that Buhl broke trail all the way to the Pass carrying a 25kg rucsac. Diemberger was carrying much the same weight. On 25 June they climbed past Kaberi Peak and set a camp at the col between it and Chogolisa's main summit. A storm pinned them in the camp on 26 June, but the next day the weather improved (as it did at Base Camp for Schmuck and Wintersteller). Buhl and Diemberger started for the summit at 4.45am. Diemberger had wanted to start earlier, but Buhl was concerned that the early morning cold might affect his right foot, as it had on Broad Peak. The weather remained fine until the pair were at about 7300m (around 350m from the summit). Clouds which had formed below then rose and enveloped them, causing the pair to turn and head down before the wind, which had driven the clouds, destroyed their tracks and made progress on the heavily corniced ridge dangerous. As Buhl had again been leading Diemberger was now in front. Diemberger felt a vibration in the snow and instinctively leapt to the right, away from the cornice. Later when Buhl did not catch him up, Diemberger searched the ridge in the now-improving visibility and saw a broken section of cornice: Buhl had left the track in the poor visibility and strayed on to the cornice which had collapsed beneath him. Diemberger estimated he had fallen at least 300m. He could see no sign of Buhl and conjectured that he had finished in a crevasse or been buried beneath the snow of an avalanche started by the collapsing cornice. Diemberger retreated to the high camp and the following day (28 June) returned to the expedition Base Camp.

Though the details of the climb and Buhl's fall are the same in the statement and Diemberger's book, there are differences over the objectives of the pair and the way in which they left Base Camp. In his book Diemberger says that it was always his and Buhl's intention to attempt Chogolisa (a fact confirmed by Buhl's diary, in which he noted on 20 June that 'Diemberger is going to set off for Chogolisa at midday', and by the conversations with Qader) but in the statement he says it was his intention only to take photographs in the upper Baltoro Glacier and, perhaps, to climb a peak. The book version has Buhl and

Diemberger agreeing that Diemberger will leave first, on the evening of 20 June, with Buhl following the next day as he had to go via the equipment dump at the base of Broad Peak to gather extra gear (timescales consistent with the entry in Buhl's diary). But the statement states that Buhl would only follow if he feels better the following day (echoing the comment of Wintersteller that Buhl had complained of still being weak on the night before his departure). The statement does not say anything about when the decision to attempt Chogolisa was made, but it is clear that it had already been made by 20 June at the latest. What Diemberger says now is that the decision to climb Chogolisa was agreed before his departure, he and Buhl deliberately keeping it a secret because of their annoyance over the Skil Brum ascent: Schmuck and Wintersteller did not arrive until after Diemberger had begun packing for Chogolisa so he did not know that they had been successful, but Qader had already told Buhl and Diemberger where the others had gone. Buhl and he decided to leave separately, Diemberger says, because that way it was easier to maintain the secret.

In his book Diemberger wonders whether, had he and Buhl been roped, the pull of the rope might have kept Buhl on track so that he would not have strayed out on to the cornice. In a recent conversation with Wintersteller another possibility was raised: had the two been roped Buhl might have pulled Diemberger off the ridge. Had that happened, Wintersteller points out, the fact that neither he nor Schmuck had any idea where the two had gone would have meant – if bad weather destroyed their tracks from Base Camp – that the disappearance of the pair would have remained a mystery until the Japanese happened upon their tent the following year. But, of course, when Wintersteller made that comment he did not know that Qader had known of the Chogolisa attempt all along. An examination of the photograph Diemberger took of the accident site also suggests another possibility. The Chogolisa ridge is not straight, a large bite having been taken out of it close to the accident site. The weather improved shortly after the cornice collapsed. As it was clearing, did Buhl vaguely see Diemberger ahead of him and, assuming that he needed to follow a straight

The label on this Wintersteller shot states 'Hermann's Grab' – Hermann's grave. It was taken during the Schmuck/Wintersteller search and shows the avalanche basin below the Chogolisa ridge into which Buhl fell.

line to him and unable to see Diemberger's tracks curving away to the right, walk directly after him and over the cornice?

The Search

On the evening of 28 June Schmuck was angry with Diemberger: 'In the evening I tell Kurt that my opinion is that he is responsible for Hermann's having been on the climb! We prepare ourselves for the departure on the following morning. Sleepless night – no wonder!' Wintersteller made no mention of this outburst, but even now is of the opinion that Buhl was not well enough to attempt Chogolisa. He says that a fit Buhl would never have strayed out over a cornice. But the history of climbing is not on his side, many good climbers having committed fatal errors in poor visibility.

The next day Schmuck and Wintersteller were up at 5am 'both tired and depressed' (Schmuck). By 7am Schmuck had already left Base Camp with the two mailrunners, having pressed both them and Qader into service as he was still hoping that the rescue of an injured Buhl was an option. He and Wintersteller had trouble persuading Diemberger to accompany them: Schmuck noted that 'Kurt is reluctant to get up, but using strong language we get him out of his tent. I admit he was very tired and also snow blind in one eye, but in the circumstances we cannot make any allowances. He has to come with us because we have no idea where exactly their so-called base camp, depot, Camp 1 and Camp 2 are, and most importantly we have to be shown where the fall occurred.' Eventually Diemberger followed with Wintersteller and Qader an hour later. Not until 5pm did the men reach the IHE Camp IV site as the snow was in dreadful condition, the trail maker, but also those following, frequently sinking hip deep into it. Two tents were erected while Wintersteller crossed the glacier to reach Buhl and Diemberger's Camp 1 to retrieve their equipment, bringing back a 20kg load. Wintersteller was again proving himself the strong man of the expedition, though in his diary he is off-hand about the effort, noting that the walk 'posed no problem as by evening the snow had frozen.'

Meanwhile, at the IHE camp site ('a flat space with a cairn of red stones: we find a stone slab into which something has been carved with a stone. The words are no longer decipherable, but it is evidence of the IHE') Schmuck was scanning the area beneath the collapsed cornice for any sign of Buhl, the mountain side now occasionally showing through the mist and cloud. Schmuck was appalled by what he saw, but also, fleetingly, hopeful: 'Only avalanche cones consisting of sheer ice are visible, they all meet in the basin at about 6300m. I think I can discern a track leading away from the right-hand lower edge and our hopes are raised. We lay out everything necessary for an early start to a rescue operation in the wildest ice I have ever seen.' Schmuck was also hopeful that the weather would be kind to them: 'It seems that the weather will turn out fine. We are astonished because the beginning of the monsoon was announced a week ago and the weather has actually been very unsettled, no good for climbing above 6000m. Today the Mustagh Tower is impressive and our much higher mountain

(Chogolisa) is glowing, surrounded by gold-rimmed evening clouds.' That night Schmuck slept outside: 'I lie in the open in my sleeping bag on the air-bed because we only brought two small tents and there are six of us.' Schmuck was also keen to be away from the others. His climbing partner and friend lay at the foot of Chogolisa, certainly injured, probably dead. Still angry with Diemberger he was best on his own.

On 30 June Schmuck was awake early: 'When the sky turns grey I look out of my sleeping bag and unfortunately see that the face is veiled, and under the mist avalanches constantly come thundering down. Despite this we [Schmuck and Wintersteller] prepare to depart. At 6am we leave the camp without a warm breakfast because there was no more fuel.' The two men left Diemberger at the camp: he was snow-blinded, and 'desperately needs time to recover' (Schmuck).

The two would-be rescuers made good progress on frozen snow, taking the right edge of the glacier flowing down from the Kaberi Pass. Schmuck's diary takes up the story: 'We repeatedly stop in order to take a good look at the face from every angle, and at the avalanche basin beneath it. There are innumerable avalanche tracks ending at snow cones varying from 10m to 100m high. There is nothing to be seen. We scanned the whole of the northern flank. Again and again we thought that Hermann could have somehow survived the fall and could possibly be somewhere working his way down now by walking, sliding or crawling. But the chances of that are small – it would be well-nigh impossible to escape from the constant avalanches. We pant and puff our way up through the ice. We get an ever better view of the basin and the terrace that leads away from it – the only entrance to the basin is heavily crevassed. The face becomes free of mist from time to time and this allows us to examine the whole track of the avalanche from the spot where the cornice broke according to our team-mate Diemberger. It is impossible that Hermann, during his fall, could have stopped on the steep flank. The slope is 25°–45° between the vertical walls, and is, in any case, partly coated in ice. Diemberger thought that he (Buhl) might be lying on the flank, but that is completely out of the question: he must have fallen 900–1000m.

The memorial to Hermann Buhl erected by the searchers.

We continued climbing until we reach a point from where we can see the terrace and the basin from all sides. The clouds and mist surrounding the mountain impede our view again and again. We are still hoping that we can reach the basin despite the avalanches falling from all sides. It is now noon and we are both suffering from the efforts of the last few weeks. Fritz has an injured shinbone while I repeatedly have a sharp pain in the chest which hinders my breathing. We have had no warm food and drink for the last two days. We watch from a height of about 5700m as another avalanche thunders into the basin, lumps of ice shooting into it like bullets, and an enormous mass of snow covering an old avalanche bed. I am certain that if we reach the basin at all we will never get out of it again. After talking it over with Fritz I make the following decision: the extraordinary danger of avalanches does not allow, at this time, an entry into the basin without the risk of sacrificing more lives. The chances of finding Hermann after three days of innumerable avalanches are very slim, well, next to zero. A further attempt in these conditions is totally pointless.'

But despite the brave decision to abandon the attempt to search the basin on foot the pair did not give up: 'We sit on our ice tower and go on searching with the binoculars as long as the light allows. Everything seems to be in vain. Slowly the clouds envelop us too and it begins to snow. It takes a while before we can pull ourselves together for the descent. Just a few hours ago we were still hoping to take Hermann down with us, but now the last glimmer of hope has left and we descend even more depressed. A further ascent in our present shape would hardly have been possible. Belaying each other we climb down. Our legs barely carry us anymore and a terrible thirst plagues us. We reach the foot of the glacier where there are iced-over ponds. We break the ice with our axes and slurp ice and water, then we lie down in the snow. Snowflakes fall on our faces – what a good and calming effect they have. But our cold backs urge us to move again, reminding us of the danger of cold in our weakened state. Fritz goes ahead – he falls through the snow at least ten times and on top of everything injures his other leg as well. Working his way out from the most impossible positions in which he finishes in the crevasses is a strain on our nerves. Will our return to camp finish in a crevasse? It almost seems so. We both fell down and had an involuntary rest when we reached the edge of the moraine and, finding ourselves next to a glacial stream, quenched our thirst. From here we are on safe ground and reach the camp after about an hour. We are greeted with questions we can hardly answer, and with disappointment. We have to accept what has happened but we don't want to believe it. Our fellow climber is missing – he has left us.' Wintersteller noted that he and Schmuck 'reach the camp at 4.30pm absolutely shattered, but nevertheless we erect a large cairn with two memorial plaques for Hermann. Marcus gives a farewell speech.'

Schmuck was overwhelmed by the loss of his friend: 'The last rays of the sun are soothingly warm while we place the stone slab on a stone pedestal and surround it with more stones. We walk dreamily all around it and there is deathly silence when I take leave of Hermann with the words: "Dear Hermann! It's not easy for us to say farewell to you. You've been a good companion to us. We don't know your last moments, but hopefully your beloved mountains haven't made it too hard for you. Rest in Chogolisa's lap. We won't forget you. We will return". An ice-axe takes the place of flowers. Then I had to go away, I couldn't hold back the tears. We stood scattered around as if we didn't belong together. We all wanted to be alone, yet we all wanted to be together – none of us should be missing.

'Meanwhile the mountains have thrown shadows over us, only the high peaks shine in the reddish yellow rays. Even 7654m Chogolisa unveils itself, with its threatening white face. Just as last night I lie in the bivouac bag tonight, my face towards Chogolisa whose summit is still glowing while down here night is already falling. The stars surround the mountains' silhouettes and I keep looking up to the ridge where Hermann took his last steps. The mountain and fate have taken him to themselves.'

Schmuck's diary for 30 June ends there, sadness having over-come any rancour, but Wintersteller's noted that after his farewell to Buhl Schmuck had again vented his anger at Diemberger, telling him that his view was that 'he [Diemberger] had blackmailed Hermann into making the attempt on the Chogolisa, and is thus indirectly responsible for his death.'

On 1 July the team walked back to Base Camp. They had no fuel and little food and so had to wait until they reached the camp before they could eat. Over the next four days the relation-ship between Schmuck and Diemberger deteriorated rapidly. At first Schmuck merely noted that Diemberger's behaviour was irritating – he ate like a wolf when they were all hungry, refused to do the washing up despite its being his turn and his having promised, then got up late when the other two were busy pack-ing – but eventually he snapped. On 3 July Wintersteller and Qader left for the equipment dump created on the inward jour-ney hoping to find the porters. Schmuck noted that Diemberger shouted a farewell from his tent, but only to Qader, ignoring the departing Wintersteller. Schmuck then wrote: 'At 10am Kurt finally comes out of his tent, but instead of helping me he takes my checklist and says cheekily: "Don't pack it in so neatly, I need to take photos of various things and I'll have to take them out again!" I don't allow him to do this, at which he tells me he is obliged to take pictures and wants a written statement from me that he doesn't have to. Such a snot-nosed brat! He couldn't be persuaded to help with the packing despite having been asked repeatedly. Instead he busied himself unnecessarily with opening already packed chests. This way he gets out of the packing. Why do I have to tolerate such a workshy individual on an expedition and one who is as cheeky as a street urchin, setting himself up as a god.' The next day, the last before the return march, Schmuck was even more vehement in his diary: 'Hakim arrives from the camp about 10am, tells us that the porters are coming and begins to make tea. Deep down I am glad. I quickly pack up our last things … As always Kurt isn't ready with his personal belongings. At my "such a lazy bastard" he flies off the handle in the presence of the porters and instead of hurrying up he angrily goes around moaning for a while, during which time I pack our tent away with the help of a porter. This was the end of my relationship with this lone wolf, this self-centred egomaniac.' That evening Schmuck noted: 'I am over the moon when I see Fritz and Qader again. Kurt sleeps alone because nobody wants to share a tent with him. That says it all – a self-imposed, wordless exclusion. He has to put up his own tent – the task will do him the world of good.'

The Return

The return to civilisation was pleasure tempered with unpleasantness and, for Schmuck, occasional throat-choking moments of grief over the loss of Hermann Buhl.

Wintersteller noted with sheer bliss the day when Ismael, the head porter, brought in two live chickens so that the party could have fresh chicken soup and, later, the purchase of four goats so that they could have fresh meat. He was ecstatic when, on 5 July, they camped at Urdokas, the first time in 65 days that they had camped on a green surface rather than snow and ice: 'We run barefoot to a river and enjoy a footbath. Marcus gathers chicory for our first fresh salad.' On 8 July, 'After crossing the tongue of the Biaho Glacier I walk several kilometres barefoot in the hot

A rose at Paiju.

sand of the riverbank, a real treat for my weary feet.' On 10 July
at the sulphur springs near Chongo he took his first bath in 78
days. Yet even Wintersteller, so phlegmatic a character, could
not ignore the atmosphere constantly enveloping the party. He
was shocked when Diemberger demanded that the three men
sign a contract which shared out the remaining equipment
between them – equipment obtained by Buhl from his employer. He was even more shocked when Diemberger declined to
help a sick porter after deciding to increase his isolation from
the party by refusing to act as team doctor.

Despite his unhappiness, Schmuck was also seized by the
pleasure of a return to warmth and colour. At Urdokas he wrote:
'how marvellous are the little blossoming white moss cushions,
yellow buttercups and the red milkwort. The smell of worm-
wood overwhelms us and we rest next to a little murmuring
stream.' He was also wistful, taking long looks back towards
Broad Peak and the other mountains of the Baltoro. He noted
when Broad Peak was visible, when it was hidden by clouds. He
noted when it re-appeared after having been hidden for a while
and when, finally, it was gone for the last time. But as with
Wintersteller he was also constantly bothered by Diemberger,
though for Schmuck the problem was less the younger man's
unwillingness to make any attempt to be part of the team than
his personal hygiene which was now, he felt, threatening himself and Wintersteller. At the sulphur springs: 'we lie in the
yearned for hot ponds and even sleep a little while in the water.
Kurt washes himself without soap just rubbing his black, dirty
skin a bit. Cleaning his teeth is out of the question. He hasn't
washed during the whole march back! He is treated as his
behaviour warrants.' A day later: 'We distance ourselves more
and more from him [Diemberger] because he is so dirty now
and probably also has lice – at least he is scratching himself as if
he had.' And the next day: 'We rest by a few hot springs. We
wash. Kurt doesn't give it a thought. What a pig – everyone is
full of dust and the risk of attracting vermin rises constantly
because of the increasing temperature.'

Diemberger seems to be completely demoralised. Qader, in
conversation, says that while before the accident Diemberger

Skinraft used during the walk out.

was offensive, now, it seemed to him, that the youngest Austrian was scared. If Qader is right, exactly what Diemberger was scared of is not clear – did he fear instant retribution from an outraged Schmuck or what the homecoming to Austria might bring, the country's legendary climber dead and he his last companion? On 12 July Machmad Ali, one of the two mailrunners and therefore a man who had helped in the search for Hermann Buhl, invited Schmuck and Wintersteller to his home in the village of Net. But Machmad, who along with many of the porters seems to have disliked Diemberger, did not want him to join the trip. Schmuck wrote 'I let him know but nevertheless he follows us like a dog and claims it must be a mistake that he hasn't been invited. Machmad's reception after being away for three months is touching. His sister and other women tearfully fling their arms around his neck. First we stay at his brother's and then at his own place. Carpets and benches are laid out for us to sit.

Then there are chickens, baratas and mulberries.' Wintersteller noted the same incident: 'We sit on benches before outspread carpets and eat chicken, baratas and mulberries. Kurt, who is not very popular with the porters either, and was not therefore invited, nevertheless, by his mere presence, forces them to give him a place at the table.'

Only when the expedition had the chance of using rafts on the swollen Braldu – offering excitement as well as the chance to save a day's walking – do Schmuck and Wintersteller finally regain any sense of real enjoyment in the trip. As usual Wintersteller was heavy on the mechanics of the raft: 'We rush over banks of coarse scree to the water where two "skinrafts" are ready for us. Thirty-six inflated sheep or goat skins tightly bound together with poles make a very secure raft. We sit on boxes in the dry while the two raftsmen, naked-bottomed, stand at the edge of the raft and steer it very skilfully along the river, which is very rough here. The skins are not absolutely water-tight so the rafts gradually sink into the water and the skins have to be reinflated on a sandbank from time to time. At the confluence with the Indus we have to cross a great stretch of water and are concerned whether there will be sufficient air in the skins – there is, and we make it, and at 7.30pm are able to sit around a proper table in a guesthouse for the first time in months.' Schmuck's recollection was a bit more wide-eyed: 'We are a bit frightened when we watch the two rafts (about 40 inflated goatskins) crossing the still very troubled river at great speed. We get on the raft with a few loads and begin our jour-ney while the porters are just taken to the other side and then have to do a two-day march. Great experience as a conclusion.'

Wintersteller's entry on the rafting (on 13 July) is the last extended entry of his diary. There is no entry at all on 14 July and then merely a series of one-line entries noting the travel itin-erary, ending with '26/07 Friday. Flight Basel – Amsterdam – Salzburg.' Schmuck was more voluble, and when the Austrians arrived in Rawalpindi he made a serious accusation against Diemberger. At Base Camp before the march back both Schmuck and Wintersteller noted that Buhl's personal property had been packed into an aluminium chest for safe keeping. Wintersteller also noted that 'We make an inventory of Hermann's things.' On 19 July Schmuck wrote: 'Kurt steals Hermann's diaries in which he is described!' This is a remarkable observation. Wintersteller does not make it and now has little to say about it.

Schmuck and Wintersteller kept diaries as a matter of course during the expedition: they were the hand-written log books that almost all Austrian climbers kept. Both men kept log books throughout their entire climbing careers and say that Buhl did the same. To support this view a Buhl diary was found by the Japanese climbers in the Chogolisa camp.

In response to my written question regarding the taking of the Buhl diaries Diemberger wrote: 'The diaries of my dear friend and ropemate I carried 1957 personally with me, so that they might not get lost on the long dangerous way home.' He also wrote: 'I gave them personally to (Frau Buhl) on return ... as I did later with his notebook from Chogolisa found by the Japanese and handed to Bonatti.'

As noted earlier, the material Horst Höfler unearthed while researching his biography of Buhl included a transcript of Buhl's expedition diary. Unsigned and undated the transcript has no direct provenance, though it was obviously typed on a different typewriter from the one which produced Buhl's reports. It was typed by a poor typist as there are many corrections. Höfler says that he did not see any hand-written diaries during his research at the Buhl home near Berchtesgaden. In his book he recounts the story Diemberger repeated to me: that the Japanese gave the diary to Walter Bonatti who gave it to Diemberger for return to Buhl's wife. But the only extract Höfler could use from that diary was the one Diemberger quoted in his book as the actual diary, or a transcript of it, were not seen. That extract is, as far as I have been able to ascertain, the only one which has ever been published from the diary found on Chogolisa.

Schmuck says that Diemberger took the Broad Peak diary because he was afraid of the comments about him it might contain. As Buhl's diary noted, Diemberger did borrow it on at least one occasion to check dates (which, of course, implies he was writing a journal of his own, something which he now denies).

If there were damning comments Diemberger would have seen them. But then, had there been damning comments Buhl might not have been so keen to pass it over. The Schmuck/ Wintersteller view is that the transcript found by Höfler is dubious and that the real diaries will never be seen, having been spirited away because of their incendiary content. It is possible we will never know the truth.

In response to my question as to why, if he saw Diemberger taking Buhl's diary he did not stop him, Schmuck's answer was simple: apart from attacking Diemberger and forcibly removing the notebooks there was little that could be done. Schmuck (and Wintersteller) say now that had they realised that the notebooks would never be seen again that is what they would have done.

Schmuck's entry regarding the incident was the final one on 19 July. Thereafter Schmuck made only one further mention of Diemberger, and that just a passing comment. Indeed, it is not possible from his diary to know even if Diemberger accompanied Wintersteller and himself on the flights back to Austria (though in fact he did). It is also not possible to confirm Qader's contention (in conversation) that he (Qader) excluded Diemberger from all the formal engagements of the team in Pakistan, these including receptions at Peshawar, Rawalpindi and Karachi, the latter involving the President of Pakistan. But it is possible to conclude that Diemberger had not only been written out of the diaries of Schmuck and Wintersteller, but out of the expedition altogether.

As he was on the outward journey, now truly a lifetime away, Schmuck was fascinated by Pakistan, noting the beauty of Peshawar and visiting the Golden Mosque and Shalimar Gardens at Lahore. His final entry was, of course, for 26 July. It ended: '10.05 take-off for the flight home. Above the clouds towards home at last! I am madly looking forward to home and family. We should arrive in Salzburg at 12.30! I can hardly wait!'

Left to right: Wintersteller, Schmuck and Diemberger with flowers presented to them on their arrival at Salzburg.

187

7

After Broad Peak

Marcus Schmuck returned to his occupation as an electrician. His enthusiasm for climbing had not diminished, but he was still restricted in the way he had been before Broad Peak, work and family limiting him to weekends and occasional longer trips. In August 1958 he and Otto Wintersteller, Fritz's brother, camped beneath the Eiger's north wall. The wall was Schmuck's major climbing ambition, but the pair had chosen the wrong year. A few days earlier a three-man team had been forced to withdraw when one of them was hit by stones. Then the weather broke. In 1958 there were no ascents of the face. Four years later Otto Wintersteller succeeded in climbing the wall, but with a new climbing partner. By then Schmuck was 37 and the climbing world was a different place. Schmuck had always climbed with friends, but his technical abilities had outstripped all of them except Hermann Buhl. With Buhl dead, Schmuck found it difficult to find a partner of equal ability who was not part of the new generation which climbed more or less full-time. He made a number of significant ascents, including some with his eldest son Christian, but as time passed he became more and more interested in the exploration which had always been a part of his life. As his family grew he was able to devote more time to expeditions. As team leader and trip organiser he climbed Mount Kenya and Kilimanjaro, the latter several times; Aconcagua and several other Andean peaks; Pik Lenin and Pik Kommunisma (7495m) in the Pamirs; Elbrus;

Camp 1, 1957.

189

several first ascents in the Hindu Kush, including that of Darab Zom (7220m) and the three peaks of Noshaq (7200m, 7400m and 7425m); Trisul (7120m) in the Garwhal Himalaya; and a new route on Mustagh Ata (7546m). Schmuck never stood on the top of another 8000m peak, but as a leader he helped many achieve their ambition to do so, his expeditions putting twelve members on the summit of Shisha Pangma and thirteen on top of Cho Oyu, though his expeditions to Gasherbrum II and Everest (north ridge) were less successful. He was still climbing at a high level until well into his sixties, though after an expedition to Nanga Parbat in 2000 he was advised by his doctor not to go to altitude again.

Fritz Wintersteller also went back to being an electrician and a weekend climber, but the enthusiasm for high hills inspired by Broad Peak led him to join Schmuck on several of his expeditions. He climbed Mount Kenya and Kilimanjaro, and Aconcagua on Schmuck-led trips. He also went to the USA with Schmuck, climbing Mount Rainier with him and Pete Schoening, the American who was one of the first pair to the summit of Gasherbrum I. Wintersteller liked the USA and returned several times, climbing again with Schoening, and also with Dee Molenaar, another member of the successful American Gasherbrum I expedition. Although his later climbs were not to the standard of those of his early years as a rock climber, Wintersteller's love of adventure has remained undiminished. In 2003 he tried his hand at sailing, crewing a boat on a long journey across the Adriatic. On his return to Salzburg from that trip he lost little time in getting back to the hills again. Attempts to talk to him about Broad Peak or his other climbs are always hampered by news that he is swimming, or off on his bike, or skiing, or just walking in the mountains. That his enthusiasm is driven by love of the mountain environment rather than a competitive urge can be seen from the fact that despite ticking off the European 4000m peaks he finished seven short of the total number. He had no desire to complete the set because as far as he was concerned the remaining seven were peaks of no beauty or interest.

Kurt Diemberger has had by far the most glittering mountaineering career of the three who came back from Broad Peak. In August 1959 he and Wolfgang Stefan completed what at first was greeted as the thirteenth ascent of the Eiger's north wall. The climb, because of the superstitions associated with the number, drew a lot of publicity. Only later was it discovered that two Germans who had disappeared during a climb in 1957 had reached the top and died on the descent. That, and a decision to accept that two climbers who had died falling from the summit ice field in 1953 had indeed climbed the face, meant that Diemberger and Stefan had actually made the fifteenth ascent. In 1960 Diemberger was a member of the predominantly Swiss team which made the first ascent of Dhaulagiri, the last of the accessible 8000ers to be climbed (Shisha Pangma in Chinese-occupied Tibet was the last 8000er to be climbed in 1964). Diemberger was one of the team of six climbers who first reached the summit (a team of two repeated the climb a few days later). Diemberger therefore shares with Hermann Buhl the distinction of having been the only climber to have been in the first teams to the top of two 8000m peaks. Later Diemberger climbed other 8000ers, including Everest, K2 and Makalu. At one point he was seen as a credible rival to Reinhold Messner in the bid to be the first man to climb all fourteen 8000ers. In 1984 he climbed Broad Peak for the second time, repeating the route the Schmuck expedition had pioneered to the top. Diemberger also became a prominent author and a photographer of the mountains, his idiosyncratic writing and excellent photography reaching a wide audience.

The Aftermath

Marcus Schmuck's book on the Broad Peak expedition was not translated into English. The English publishing world had been keen on translating mountaineering books in the early years of climbing on the high hills, particularly those which dealt with expeditions to the 8000m peaks. Before the 1939–45 War the books on the German expeditions to Nanga Parbat and

Kangchenjunga had been translated, as had that on the French expedition to the Karakoram (although that on the IHE Gasherbrum trip had not). In the post-War era Herzog's book on Annapurna had been a best-seller, perhaps persuading the publishing world to risk the translation of the official books of the expeditions to K2, Makalu and Cho Oyu. And, of course, Nanga Parbat, where both Herrligkoffer's official book and Hermann Buhl's account of the climb (part of his autobiography) were translated. By the time Manaslu was climbed the mood had changed. There was no translation of the Japanese book, neither was there one of Moravec's account of the Gasherbrum II success. The Lhotse ascent (which came between these climbs) was translated because the Swiss made the second ascent of Everest on the same expedition. Broad Peak followed Gasherbrum II and was also ignored. Later the expedition book on Dhaulagiri was translated, probably because it was both the last 8000er (with Shisha Pangma being potentially off-limits forever) and had a reputation as one of the most challenging, an idea reinforced by the failure of half-a-dozen expeditions in the 1950s.

As a consequence of this lack of a book, the public perception of the Broad Peak expedition in the English-speaking world was based largely on the writings of Kurt Diemberger, and in particular his account of the climb in his first book to be published in English (*Summits and Secrets*, 1971). It can be argued that the number and popularity of Diemberger's writings in the German-speaking world also overwhelmed Schmuck's account which had, by comparison, a modest print run. By 1971 the legend of Hermann Buhl had grown. Each year that passed seemed to enhance the tale of his genius. Buhl died at the apogee of his career. Despite Bonatti's climbs on the Dru and the Grand Capucin, Buhl was still the most famous climber in the world. The climbing of Broad Peak and the tragedy of Chogolisa confirmed his fame. For pop stars, a tragic death at the height of success (and such deaths are always tragic – how could it be otherwise when the Reaper harvests a young life, whatever the circumstances) is the key to lasting fame. Spared the elbowing aside by newer, more credible rivals, the descent into the mediocrity of middle age, or spiteful, patronising commentators if the descent is not fast or far enough, the sharp flame of a short career is oxygenated by an army of willing fans. Something similar happened to Hermann Buhl. Nanga Parbat had established a reputation time could never erase. Buhl left Munich as both hero and legend, but he was too competitive not to have returned to sing the new songs needed to maintain his position. Death prevented the possibility of failure, sealing everlasting success.

As the last man to see Buhl alive it was inevitable that Kurt Diemberger's account of the Chogolisa climb would be sought after. Add the romance of Buhl's last summit, reached as the sun went down, the fact that the summit was of one of the last 8000ers to be climbed and Buhl's second, and you have an unbeatable combination.

Perhaps because of this demand or perhaps more consciously, Kurt Diemberger became a custodian of the Buhl legend. Diemberger is keen to ensure that his version of his climbs is the one that is seen in print. In 1960 Diemberger joined the Swiss expedition to Dhaulagiri. Diemberger's account is that he was invited to join the expedition. In the official book of the expedition (*Erfolg am Dhaulagiri*, 1960, published in English as *The Ascent of Dhaulagiri*, 1961) the team leader, Max Eiselin, has a different version, saying that Diemberger visited him one day and asked to be allowed to join the expedition. Eiselin writes that he was 'glad to welcome' Diemberger because of his considerable Himalayan experience, as well as his talents as a writer and photographer. Of the expedition, Eiselin writes that in his effort to get to the summit first Diemberger disobeyed his (Eiselin's) orders on climbing towards the top camp, later saying 'on Broad Peak they beat me to it, although I had done all the hard work.' The decision infuriated the expedition doctor (Georg Hajdukiewicz), who felt that Diemberger was not fit enough to ascend so far so fast (and, implicitly, was threatening the success of the expedition by risking the need for an assisted evacuation). The decision also infuriated the deputy leader (Ernst Forrer) who was one of the two climbing with Diemberger. Diemberger put distance between himself and the others so that Forrer would not be able to order him to stop. At Camp 5 nine men huddled into two tents, an unrealistic situation which might have resulted in a failed summit bid had not three decided to descend. In most first-hand accounts the decision by those three (a fortuitous one as it turned out, as one of them developed symptoms of AMS on the descent) followed a furious row provoked by Diemberger. The next day at Camp 6, six men spent the night in one tent, one of the two Sherpas eventually sleeping outside after refusing an order from Diemberger to cook all night because he had already cooked non-stop for many hours. The next day the six men made the first ascent of Dhaulagiri, Diemberger, Albin Schelbert and Sherpa Nawang Dorje reaching the top first.

By contrast to the official account of the climb, Diemberger's version (in *Summits and Secrets*) of the expedition makes little mention of these critical issues, nor of any desire to be first to the top. The only acknowledgement of the differences in the two versions is Diemberger's enthusiasm for signing copies of Eiselin's official book, adding 'Please compare this report with *"Summits and Secrets"* which gives the real story!'

I encountered Diemberger's enthusiasm for the 'real' story personally in 2000 when I wrote a history of climbing on the 8000m peaks. The book was timed for publication on 3 June 2000, the 50th anniversary of the first ascent of Annapurna. I had found Fritz Wintersteller's photograph of Marcus Schmuck on the summit of Broad Peak, an image which had, as far as could be judged, never appeared in an English-language magazine or book. But the publisher also wanted to use the famous image of Buhl on the summit in the dying daylight. Diemberger was contacted about that image and others which might also be used, of Dhaulagiri and his other 8000m climbs. He insisted on the publisher signing a contract (the only supplier of photographs who did). One clause noted that he must be shown any pages which referred to him or his climbs. He would, the clause said, point out errors of fact to the author, but the decision regarding changes would remain with the author. The clause was important as I was already aware of Diemberger's desire for control over all material related to expeditions in which he participated. The clause meant that I would not have to change the text if the issues noted were matters of opinion. I submitted the text and book production trundled on in the usual frustratingly slow way. I saw the final page proofs. When the books finally arrived they were different, the accounts of the Broad Peak (in particular) and Dhaulagiri climbs having been altered without my knowledge or permission. Late in the production process the publisher had received a note from Diemberger. Unless the text was changed and unless references were made in the text to his books he was withdrawing permission for the use of his photographs. Perhaps remembering the contract, Diemberger's note stated that use of the photographs without text changes would result in his (Diemberger) suing the publisher for illegal use and breach of copyright. With printing only days away the publishers were in trouble. They were aware that I would probably not accept changes to the text and that I had been adamant that no book titles should be mentioned in the text as the book included a bibliography. They were aware that I knew about the Diemberger contract and its 'no change' clause. But they were aware too that Diemberger did not make idle threats. In breach of their contract with me they changed the text, deciding against telling me before publication in case I decided to exercise my own rights. I was left to field a letter of complaint from Marcus Schmuck, rather a mild one in the circumstances, and a more stinging rebuke from Fritz Wintersteller.

There are few of us who would not, given the opportunity, move the spotlight of history so that it shone closer to us or so that certain truths were ushered towards the shadows. In his version of the Dhaulagiri ascent Diemberger does that, but Eiselin's version adjusts the balance. With the Broad Peak climb the situation is different because there has been no balancing view (in English, or available to most readers of German as Diemberger's books have controlled the market). The imbalance becomes even more critical when the custody of Hermann Buhl's legend is added to the mix.

Eiselin says that he was glad to have Diemberger along because of his Himalayan experience, despite the expedition being nominally Swiss. But there was no shortage of Swiss climbers with big mountain experience – the Swiss had climbed Everest and Lhotse just five years before – and if nationality was no barrier there were the members of Moravec's 1959 Dhaulagiri expedition who had the extra advantage of having explored Eiselin's chosen route to 7800m. The death of a climber in tragic circumstances resulted in a long delay on that expedition: without that delay the mountain might well have been climbed. Moravec's team was Austrian, but had not included any of the surviving Broad Peak trio.

In considering Eiselin's decision it is legitimate to wonder whether it was based on the talismanic name of Hermann Buhl. Diemberger's writing occasionally revolves around Buhl, the Broad Peak summit climb and Chogolisa accident being told and retold. In *Summits and Secrets* Diemberger's account of Dhaulagiri quotes at length from his expedition diary, following the climb from start to summit. The Broad Peak chapter of the same book uses no diary material and concentrates almost exclusively on the summit climb with Buhl, and on Chogolisa.

In 1984 Diemberger climbed Broad Peak again. Then, in 1986, he survived the events on K2 which cost thirteen climbers their lives. The opening text photo of Diemberger's book on the K2 tragedy (published in English as *The Endless Knot*) is of Hermann Buhl on Broad Peak in 1957 and many pages are given over to a restatement of the 1957 summit climb, the pretext being the 1984 repetition of the Broad Peak ascent and Buhl's claimed desire to traverse K2 (which seems never to have been mentioned during the Broad Peak expedition, at least in the hearing of Schmuck or Wintersteller, or to have found its way into Buhl's writings). What is significant is the extent to which Marcus Schmuck and Fritz Wintersteller are reduced to bit-part players. They are barely mentioned – check the index, a handful of entries between them with those for Buhl reaching a quarter column. The repetitions of inaccuracies or, at best, unsubstantiated assertions, continues: the repeated suggestion that it was Buhl's expedition and he asked Schmuck to join him; the suggestion that Buhl invited Diemberger to join; the idea that it was Diemberger who did all the hard work, but was then cruelly denied the chance of reaching the summit first; that from the Forepeak Diemberger could see that the true summit lay at the other end of the final ridge.

Diemberger's claim to the Buhl legend is, in one sense, hardly surprising. The Buhl name sells: although Marcus Schmuck called his book *Broad Peak 8047m*, he subtitled it *Meine Bergfahrten mit Hermann Buhl*. But the claim has served to distort the Broad Peak climb, obscuring the truth of a superb and revolutionary ascent. Broad Peak was not climbed by Hermann Buhl and Kurt Diemberger, and two others. It could be better argued that it was climbed because of the vision of Marcus Schmuck and Hermann Buhl and that two others were lucky enough to be able to share their vision. Of the actual ascent it could be argued that Broad Peak was climbed by Marcus Schmuck and Fritz Wintersteller, and two others (and even, perhaps, by the indomitable Wintersteller and three others). In reality it was climbed by four Austrians, two of whom will, hopefully, now finally join their team-mates as recipients of the credit they deserve.

Ascents of Broad Peak

Data from Eberhard Jurgalski and with thanks also to Xavier Eguskitza

Note that some of the ascents listed below may only have been to Forepeak. Definitive details on the actual point reached are occasionally hard to obtain.

All ascents have been along the line of the first ascent (West Spur to Wind Gap/Broad Col, then over the Forepeak and along the summit ridge) except where stated. Female climbers marked (f). Climbers marked (†) died during their descent from the summit.

09/06/57
Hermann Buhl (Austria), Kurt Diemberger (Austria),
Marcus Schmuck (Austria), Frtiz Wintersteller (Austria)

08/88/77
Kazuhisa Noro (Japan), Takashi Ozaki (Japan),
Yoshiyuki Tsuji (Japan)

04/06/78
Yannick Seigneur (France), Georges Bettembourg (France)
Bettembourg did not reach the main summit and claimed that Seigneur also failed. This is strongly denied by Seigneur, despite his once having admitted in an article that he returned from the low point midway between the Forepeak and the main summit.

05/08/81
Manuel Hernández (Spain), Enric Pujol (†)(Spain)

23/07/82
Georg Bachler (Austria), Ralph Bärtle (Germany),
Peter Gloggner (Germany), Hans Kirchberger (Germany), Konrad
Lewankowski (Germany), Walter Lösch (Austria), Werner Sucher
(Austria)

30/07/82
Jerzy Kukuczka (Poland), Wojciech Kurtyka (Poland)

02/08/82
Mohammad Sher Khan (Pakistan), Reinhold Messner (Italy), Nazir
Ahmad Sabir (Pakistan)

25/06/83
Jean Afanassieff (France), Roger Baxter-Jones (UK),
Andrew Parkin (UK), Alan Rouse (UK)

28/06/83
Douglas Scott (UK), Stephen Sustad (USA)

30/06/83
Fredi Graf (Switzerland), Erhard Loretan (Switzerland),
Krystyna Palmowska (f)(Poland), Marcel Ruedi (Switzerland),
Stefan Wörner (Switzerland)

In reaching the summit Krystyna Palmowska completed the first
wholly female ascent of an 8000m peak. She and fellow Pole Anna
Czerwinska, after a semi-alpine ascent with two camps, reached the
Forepeak. Unfortunately Czerwinska was forced to stop at the col
between the Forepeak and the main summit, Palmowska continuing to
the main summit alone.

02/07/83
Pierre Morand (Switzerland),
Jean-Claude Sonnenwyl (Switzerland)

26/06/84
Manuel Barrios (Colombia), Louis Deuber (Switzerland), Richard
Franzl (Austria), Thomas Hägler (Switzerland), Andreas Reinhard
(Switzerland)

27/06/84
Giovanni Calcagno (Italy), Alberto Enzio (Italy),
Tullio Vidoni (Italy)

13/07/84
Giovanni Calcagno (Italy)(2nd ascent), Karl Hub (Germany),
Rüdiger Schleypen (Germany), Tullio Vidoni (Italy)(2nd ascent)

14/07/84
Walenty Fiut (Poland), Janusz Majer (Poland),
Ryszard Pawlowski (Poland), Krzysztof Wielicki (Poland), Hans
Zebrowski (Germany)

17/07/84
Jerzy Kukuczka (Poland) (2nd ascent),
Wojciech Kurtyka (Poland)(2nd ascent)
18/07/84
Kurt Diemberger (Austria)(2nd ascent), Julie Tullis (f)(UK)

08/08/84
Reinmar Joswig (Germany), Robert Schauer (Austria)

1984 was the year of the repeat ascents, all five of the second ascents of Broad Peak recorded to date occurring then. The second ascent of Calcagno and Vidoni was the most remarkable, occurring just sixteen days after their first ascent. Their first climb had been queried by other members of the team and so they did it again to prove a point.

The ascent by Kukuczka and Kurtyka in 1982 had been unauthorised as they had, rightly, considered that Pakistani permission to climb minor peaks as part of the acclimatisation programme for a K2 expedition would not extend to another 8000m peak. The pair therefore returned in 1984. Their plan was to climb the, still unclimbed, south ridge to the main summit, then to traverse over the Central and North summits. Their alpine attempt on the south ridge failed because very hard climbing was absorbing too much time. They also had their tent ripped from over their heads by falling rocks. They therefore climbed the easier west ridge of the North summit, continuing along the ridge to the Central summit. The pair then descended to Broad Col from where they followed the original route over the Forepeak to the main summit, finally descending the original route. The climb required four bivouacs.

On his second ascent Kurt Diemberger noted that the climb from Broad Col to the Forepeak was much harder than it had been in 1957.

31/07/85
Fayyaz Hussain (Pakistan), Zahid Mahmood (Pakistan),
Jawad Pirzada (Pakistan)

12/08/85
Shin Kashu (Japan), Riichi Nishizutsumi (Japan),
Tsuneo Shigehiro (Japan), Tetsuya Toyama (Japan),
Seishi Wada (Japan), Munehiko Yamamoto (Japan)

20/06/86
Soro Dorotei (Italy), Marino Giacometti (Italy),
Martino Moretti (Italy)

21/06/86
Beda Fuster (Switzerland), Markus Prechtl (Germany),
Diego Wellig (Switzerland), Peter Wörgötter (Austria),
Rolf Zemp (Switzerland)

22/06/86
Josef Rakoncaj (Czech Rep)

23/06/86
Heinrich Koch (Germany), Jochen Labisch (Germany)

07/07/86
Sebastian Hölzl (Austria), Fritz Schreinmoser (Austria)

28/07/86
Bogdan Biščak (Slovenia), Viktor Grošelj (Slovenia)

29/07/86
Tomislav Česen (Slovenia), Rado Fabjan (Slovenia),
Tomaž Jamnik (Slovenia), Andrej Štremfelj (Slovenia),
Marija Štremfelj (f)(Slovenia)

30/07/86
Pavle Kozjek (Slovenia)

04/08/86
Dušan Jelinčič (Slovenia), Silvo Karo (Slovenia),
Matevž Lenarčič (Slovenia), Mojmir Štangelj (Slovenia)

16/08/86
Brian Agnew (Australia), Jonathan Chester (Australia),
Patrick Cullinan (Australia), Michael Dacher (Germany),
Karl Fassnacht (Germany), Gabriele Hupfauer (f)(Germany), Siegfried
Hupfauer (Germany), Peter Lambert (Australia),
Terry McCullagh (Australia), Michael Rheinberger (Australia), James
Van Gelder (Australia), Zacharias Zaharias (Australia)

29/05/87
Norbert Joos (Switzerland)

07/06/87
Bruno Honegger (Switzerland), Ernst Müller (Switzerland)

27/06/88
Sachi Matsumoto (f)(Japan), Kunimitsu Sakai (Japan),
Masato Sasaki (Japan), Kenji Shimakata (Japan)

01/08/88
Claudio Schranz (Italy)

12/08/88
Junji Saito (Japan), Mamoru Taniguchi (Japan)

09/09/88
Luís Gómez (Spain), Carles Vallès (Spain)

12/07/91
Keijiro Hayasaka (Japan), Iwao Ogasawara (Japan),
Masanori Sato (Japan), Taro Tanigawa (Japan),
Toshimasa Yawata (Japan)

16/07/91
Robin Beadle (UK), Ramón Blanco (Spain), Alan Hinkes (UK)

30/07/91
Masami Abe (Japan), Hirofumi Konishi (Japan),

Taeko Yamanoi (f)(Japan), Yasushi Yamanoi (Japan),
Tetsuaki Yoshimura (Japan)

02/08/92
David Hambly (UK), Constantin Lacatusu (Romania),
Eudald Martínez (Spain), Scott McKee (USA),
Pedro Rodríguez (Spain), Antonio Tapiador (Spain)

06/07/93
Marco Bianchi (Italy), Christian Kuntner (Italy)

07/07/93
Albert Brugger (Italy), Sergio De Leo (Italy),
Fausto De Stefani (Italy), Tobias Heymann (Germany),

21/07/93
Sarwar Khan (Pakistan), Rajab Shah (Pakistan),
Masakatsu Tamura (Japan), Nobuhiro Tsuji (Japan)

29/07/93
Abele Blanc (Italy), Sergio Martini (Italy),
Nima Temba II (Nepal), Ali Raza (Pakistan)

24/08/93
Shinsuke Ezuka (Japan), Kazuya Mino (Japan),
Takashi Nakamura (Japan), Osamu Tanabe (Japan),
Kenichi Uchida (Japan)

21/06/94
Hans Kammerlander (Italy)
02/07/94
Göran Kropp (Sweden)

03/07/94
Alessandro Busca (Italy)

09/07/94
Carlos Carsolio (Mexico)
Carsolio soloed a new route to the right of the original route, climbing
over Pt6230. His third bivouac was below the headwall to the
Forepeak at his route's junction with the original route, where Camp

III of commercial climbs is usually placed. Bad weather then forced him to retreat. Later Carsolio climbed the original route to Camp III, that route having been prepared by other expeditions, and his earlier bivouac site. Here his stove exploded burning down his tent and removing his moustache. Undeterred by either loss he climbed the headwall directly to the Forepeak, then followed the original route to the top. He reached the summit as night fell and returned to Camp III where he was helped by a Basque expedition.

10/07/94
Emmanuel Morin (France)

23/07/94
Bo Christensen (Denmark), Francisco Ibarbia (Spain),
Jan Mathorne (Denmark)

12/07/95
Ángel Abrego (Spain), Josema Casimiro (Spain),
Lee Jeong-Hyun (S Korea), Juan Oiarzabal (Spain),
Park Hyun-Jae (†)(S Korea), Park Shin-Young (S Korea),
Um Hong-Gil (S Korea)

20/07/95
Toru Hattori (Japan), Toshiyuki Kitamura (Japan),
Masafumi Todaka (Japan)
(Followed the Polish route over the North and Central summits to the main summit)

13/08/95
Jeff Alzner (USA), Ang Dorje II (Nepal),
Shelley Ballard (f)(Canada), Michael Boyle (USA),
Dawa Galjen (Nepal), Jorg Ehrlich (Germany),
Christine Feld-Boskoff (f)(USA), Scott Fischer (USA),
Peter Goldman (USA), Rob Hess (USA),
Jörg Leupold (Germany), Aaron Lish (USA),
Lobsang Jangbu (Nepal), Iván Loredo (Mexico),
Andrew McKinlay (Canada), Waldemar Soroka (Poland),
Markus Walter (Germany), Frederick Ziel (USA)

20/07/96
Han Dong-Keu (†)(S Korea), Yang Jae-Mo (†)(S Korea)

13/07/97
Alberto Iñurrategi (Spain), Felix Iñurrategi (Spain)

16/07/97
Arjun Tamang (Nepal), Dawa Tsering II (Nepal),
Masashi Fukumoto (Japan), Hiroshi Iwazaki (Japan),
Mitsuyoshi Sato (Japan), Fumie Yoshida (f)(Japan),
Hideki Yoshida (Japan), Saichi Yanase (Japan)

19/07/97
Jared Coburn (USA), Barry Montoya (USA),
Manuel Schneider (Germany), Tony Tonsing (USA)

20/07/97
Fumiaki Goto (Japan), Nawang Dorje (Nepal),
Yoshio Ogata (Japan)

07/08/97
A Lock (Australia)

09/08/97
Juan-Carlos Cirera (Spain)

05/07/98
Robert Bösch (Switzerland), Karl Kobler (Switzerland),
Iván Vallejo (Ecuador)

16/07/99
Ralf Dujmovits (Germany), Gunter Hafele (Austria),
Qudrat Ali (Pakistan), Xabier Rozas (Spain),
Josef von Rotz (Switzerland)

17/07/99
Peter Fessler (Austria), Eduard Koblmüller (Austria)

26/07/00
Hidetoshi Kurahashi (Japan), Masahide Matsumoto (Japan)

29/07/00
Hideji Nazuka (Japan)

30/07/00
Nisar Hussain (Pakistan), Kang Seong-Gyu (S Korea),
Kim Hyoung-Woo (S Korea), Kazuyoshi Kondo (Japan),
Lee Hyun-Jo (S Korea), Oh Hee-Joon (S Korea),
Park Young-Seok (S Korea), Toshiaki Yano (Japan)

31/07/00
Zoltán Ács (Hungary), László Mécs (Hungary)

22/07/01
Paul Barry (USA), David Hart (USA)

23/07/01
Petko Totev (Bulgaria), Stanymir Zhelyazkov (Bulgaria)

15/07/03
Alexander Chicón (Spain), Dawa Wangchuk (Nepal),
Han Wang-Yong (S Korea), Kim Woong-Sik (S Korea),
Jean-Christophe Lafaille (France), Mingma Dorje (Nepal),
Simone Moro (Italy), Iñaki Otxoa de Olza (Spain),
Ra Kwan-Ju (S Korea), Edmund Viesturs (USA)

In 1997 Ed Viesturs climbed Broad Peak on his way to a personal goal of climbing all fourteen 8000m peaks. Those who summited the following day noticed that his tracks ended at the Forepeak and questioned him about it. Viesturs was later to admit in print that he had not made it to the main summit. Despite this he did not return to Broad Peak until 2003. That year he climbed Nanga Parbat, leaving only Annapurna for the completion of his set. But as he was resting at Nanga Base Camp he was e-mailed by someone asking him if, as he was now in the Karakoram, he was going to reach Broad Peak's true summit. This does not seem to have been part of his plan, but he immediately went to the Baltoro. On reaching the Forepeak again he found a group of South Koreans and their Sherpa companions celebrating. When he asked why he was told that it was a joint celebration: they had climbed Broad Peak and one of their number (Han Wang-Yong) had just become the eleventh person (and the third South Korean) to complete the fourteen 8000ers. Viesturs pointed out that the celebration was premature as the main summit was still an hour away. To their credit, the South Koreans accompanied Viesturs to the real top.

16/07/03
Dmitri Chumakov (Kazahkstan), Vassili Pivtsov (Kazahkstan),
Maksut Zhumayev (Kazahkstan)

17/07/03
Sergei Bogomolov (Russia), Sergei Lavrov (Kazahkstan),
Vassili Litsinov (Kazahkstan), Alexei Raspopov (Kazahkstan)

18/07/03
Ricardo Guerrero (Spain), Radek Jaroš (Czech Rep),
Petr Masek (Czech Rep), Martin0 Minařík (Czech Rep),
Jorge Palacio (Spain), Denis Urubko (Kazahkstan)

08/08/03
Romano Benet (Italy), Nives Meroi (f)(Italy),
Luca Vuerich (Italy)
Benet, Meroi and Vuerich climbed Gasherbum I, Gasherbrum II and
Broad Peak in 20 days (19/7 GII, 26/7 GI, 8/8 BP), one of the few
ascents of three 8000m peaks in one year. The same feat had been
accomplished in 1983 by Loretan and Ruedi in fifteen days and by
Sonnenwyl in seventeen days. In 1985, Eric Escoffier completed the
much more difficult trio of GII, GI and K2 in twenty-one days.

27/07/04
Paul Walters (Australia), Michael Parker (Australia), Jamie
McGuiness (New Zealand), Khadi Mehdi (Iran)

Broad Peak statistics

There have been 268 ascents by 263 climbers, 5 climbers having completed two ascents each. 10 of the summiteers have been women. 18
climbers have died on Broad Peak, 4 of them while descending from
the summit.

Broad Peak Central

In 1975 a Polish team climbed Broad Peak's Central, or Middle, summit, a team of six setting out for the summit on 28 July. The route was as for the 1957 climb to the Austrian Camp 1, then a line to the left. Two further camps were established, the last at 7200m below Broad Col. The Poles then climbed to Broad Col and followed the Middle summit's final ridge. As the Col was reached in late afternoon, one of the six decided to retreat to the top camp. The remaining five climbed on, overcoming two major obstacles to reach what they believed, correctly, to be the summit plateau. By now it was late (past 7pm) and snow had begun to fall. The men sheltered behind a rocky section of ridge from where Kazimierz Glazek went on his own to see if they really were at the top. He was joined a few minutes later by Janusz Kulis. At about 7.30pm, the visibility improved momentarily and the two could see that they were on a high point. Their colleagues were about 40m away and a few metres lower. The two men hurriedly built a cairn and returned to the others. All five then started an arduous descent.

During the descent the weather worsened, forcing the climbers to move on to the north-east face to avoid a violent blizzard. There, Bohdan Nowaczyk, the last man on an abseil, was killed when the rope anchor failed. Without a rope the four survivors were forced to bivouac. The next morning a search failed to find their companion or the rope and they tied slings together to form a makeshift line. The appalling weather made the descent painfully slow and another bivouac was inevitable. While searching for a suitable spot Andrzej Sikorski slipped, knocking Marek Kesicki and summiteer Kulis off. Only Kulis survived the fall, he and Glazek eventually making it back to the expedition's top camp. Both were frostbitten, Kulis subsequently losing most of his toes.

During their traverse of Broad Peak's three summits Jerzy Kukuczka and Wojtek Kurtyka found the summit cairn built by Glazek and Kulis and were able to confirm it stood on the actual summit. Despite the fact that technically only the cairn-builders touched the summit, the Polish climbing press has, rightly, claimed that all five members of the summit team reached the top.

Broad Peak North

The first ascent of the north peak was made by Kukuczka and Kurtyka during their three-peak traverse.